PREHISTORIC COOKING

Best Wishes

Jacqui Wood

PREHISTORIC COOKING

JACQUI WOOD

TEMPUS

First published 2001
Reprinted in 2007

Tempus Publishing is an imprint of NPI Media Group

Tempus Publishing Ltd
Cirencester Road, Chalford
Stroud, Gloucestershire GL6 8PE
www.tempus-publishing.com

© Jacqui Wood, 2001, 2007

The right of Jacqui Wood to be identified as the Author of this work has been asserted by her in accordance with the Copyrights, Designs and Patents Act 1988.

All rights reserved. No part of this book may be reprinted or reproduced or utilised in any form or by any electronic, mechanical or other means, now known or hereafter invented, including photocopying and recording, or in any information storage or retrieval system, without the permission in writing from the Publishers.

British Library Cataloguing in Publication Data.
A catalogue record for this book is available from the British Library.

isbn 978 0 7524 1943 5

Typesetting and origination by NPI Media Group
Printed and bound in Great Britain

Contents

Acknowledgements		6
List of illustrations		7
Preface		11
1	Prehistory	13
2	The hunter-gatherers	17
3	The first farmers	27
4	The Bronze Age	33
5	The Iron Age	47
6	Bread	63
7	Dairy	75
8	Meat, fish and vegetable stews	87
9	Cooking with hot stones	95
10	Clay-baked foods	111
11	Salt and the seashore menu	119
12	Peas, beans and lentils	127
13	Herbs and spices	133
14	Vegetables	141
15	Yeast, wines, beer and teas	155
16	Sweets and puddings	167
Glossary		174
Further reading		187
Index		189

Acknowledgements

I would like to thank Richard, Sue, Kif and Jean for helping me with the final draft of this book.

Photographs by Jacqui Wood and Kif Wood

Maps by Jacqui Wood

Reconstruction drawings by John Dimery

List of illustrations

Text figures

1. Estimated Mesolithic coastline around Mounts Bay and the Scilly Isles
2. An estimate of the coastline approx. 10,000 years ago
3. An estimate of the coastline approximtely 8,400 years ago
4. The density of Mesolithic forests
5. An example of 'beaver art'
6. An example of a primitive trackway
7. The Tybrind Vig boat
8. Two Mesolithic hunters
9. Iron Age settlement
10. An 'Ice Man' reconstruction
11. A log boat
12. A sprang frame
13. A typical bronze sword
14. Reconstructions of Bronze Age funerary urns
15. Drawing of a bronze couch
16. Stage one of making a furnace in which to smelt iron
17. Stage two: the smelting of the iron ore
18. The invasion of Mona
19. Bread dough
20. A Bronze Age quern
21. A bucket of bog butter
22. The Fogou at Carn Euny
23. Sticks used to whisk cream into butter
24. The first stage of butter making after making the stick balloon whisk
25. The second stage of butter making
26. The third stage of butter making
27. Nettle leaf-covered cheese
28. A basket made from Bog Myrtle for keeping soft cheese
29. A pot with milk into which hot stones have been placed
30. Beef and bread dough
31. Granite stones being heated
32. Bread-wrapped beef being covered with hot stones

List of illustrations

33	A mat and soil cover the stones
34	Two day-old bread casings
35	The famous gatehouse at Biskupin in Poland
36	Some beef ready to be wrapped in grass
37	A water pit
38	A typical days cooking at Biskupin festival
39	Duck stuffed with blackberries and baked in clay
40	Stage one of clay baking trout
41	Stage two of clay baking trout
42	Stage three of clay baking trout
43	Stage four of clay baking trout
44	The carp ready to eat
45	Sea lettuce and curd cheese fritters
46	The common carrageen
47	Rock samphire
48	Sea beet and cheese fritters
49	Fat hen in seed
50	A burdock plant
51	Mild brown ale
52	Crab apples, blackberries and myrtle leaves
53	Fruit bread

Colour plates

1. A type of marshy landscape familiar to the Mesolithic people
2. The remains of a Bronze Age lake settlement
3. A Beaker pot
4. Another Beaker pot, without the handle
5. A gold lunulae
6. Modern day St Michael's Mount
7. An example of a Baltic boat
8. A typical Bronze Age round house
9. Two Lithuanian women making copies of lime bark buckets
10. Lamb stew
11. Examples of typical textiles from Iron Age Europe
12. Querning grain into flour at Chysauster
13. A large clome bread oven
14. A Manx Loughton, the type of sheep kept in prehistory
15. Smoked fish stew
16. Honey-covered ham
17. King Carp stuffed with plums
18. Pilchards
19. Winkles
20. Some fish being smoked over a hot fire
21. Sweet bean cakes
22. Ramsons
23. Spring salad ingredients
24. Gorse flowers
25. Jack-by-the-hedge
26. Elderberries
27. Blackberries and peas

Preface

As you can imagine, writing a cookery book about a period that has no written records might be considered an impossible task. The only factual information that we have about the food eaten by our ancestors comes in the form of bone remains and some charred grains from their rubbish dumps (middens), the contents of various well-preserved bog bodies and food traces from prehistoric pots. There is also good evidence from some wetland sites, such as the Neolithic and Bronze Age lake villages of Switzerland. Due to the waterlogged conditions of these sites, food remains are very well preserved and show the abundance of wild fruits available to these people. Pollen analysis is another method by which archaeologists can discover which plants were growing at the time in the area of an excavated site. In addition, classical historians sometimes mention the type of foods that the prehistoric barbarians — 'The Celts' — preferred. Interesting though this is, it does not really give us the exact combination of ingredients that might have been put together for a meal.

We need to employ a different approach from that of merely itemising the bone remains from rubbish dumps, or making a catalogue of the pollens of plants known to be in the vicinity of a prehistoric house. I do not believe that people have changed so very much since prehistoric times as one might imagine — what seems logical to us today was probably equally obvious to the people of ancient societies. Nothing is new when it comes to surviving on our planet; skills are constantly being re-invented throughout the ages, and then forgotten again when no longer required.

So I have approached this book from the viewpoint: 'What would I do with the food ingredients that we know were available to these people?' I don't see why we seem to assume that a taste for flavour is a new skill that was suddenly acquired with the coming of the written word and the Roman Empire. I have taken into account the seasonal aspect of some foods; for instance, eggs would have come from any bird, rather than just hens, and would not have been available in the autumn or winter. We know of some ancient cooking techniques, such as the clay baking of food and cooking in water pits heated with fire-stones. Throw in some quotations from the classical historians and, by paying attention to detail, you have as good an attempt as is possible to recreate the food that was eaten in prehistory.

Although archaeology can show that all of the ingredients are known to have been available in prehistoric times, I cannot prove that *any* of these recipes would have been used — it is also the case that no one can prove that they were not.

At the beginning of this book the different periods of prehistory are described to give some background knowledge of the prehistoric peoples who are being talked about. With this book I hope to bring these periods alive by trying to imagine what it was really like to live then. The book is divided into chapters containing different food types — just the same as a modern cookery book. Each chapter has an introduction that details the background knowledge that archaeology has gleaned from excavations or from classical sources. The book is also intended as a manual on recreating the type of food that our prehistoric ancestors could have eaten. There is information about food sources that can be gathered from the wild (without damaging the environment or poisoning yourself). It instructs on how to recreate ancient cooking techniques such as clay baking foods. All of the recipes are simple to make and, where wild plants might be difficult to find, I have provided the nearest modern alternative. It is a book that will inform and, hopefully, give you lots of fun in recreating the meals. A summer barbecue need no longer be limited to depressing supermarket sausages on a gas barbecue. Why not try a fish wrapped in grasses and clay, and baked in a fire pit at the end of your garden? Why not wash it down with some prehistoric wine or beer?

As you experiment for yourselves with the ingredients in the book, you will have just as much chance of rediscovering a real prehistoric recipe, as anyone else. The past does not just belong to the professional archaeologist or university academic, it belongs to all of us.

1 Prehistory

What do we mean when we say something is prehistoric? Literally, it means 'before written history'. So at varying periods throughout the world's history *all* cultures have been 'prehistoric' until their development of the written word. Using this definition, the bushmen of the Kalahari and many other 'primitive' cultures in different parts of the world are prehistoric even today. They employ a verbal tradition to pass down knowledge from one generation to another in the form of stories and legends. This is their only facility for finding out about important events in their culture's formation. Stories could exist to warn people about poisonous types of plants by saying that a bad spirit dwells in them and that they are best left alone. The stories might tell of great migrations from distant lands because of drought or conflict with more dominant cultures. There is a quotation by the Roman historian, Pliny the Elder, which mentions a people who lived in the desert beyond the Atlas mountains. He wrote about these people living in houses made of blocks of salt:

> the Amantes . . . They build their houses of blocks of salt quarried out of their mountains like stone. From these it is a journey of seven days in a south-westerly quarter to the cave dwellers, with whom our only intercourse is the trade in the precious stones imported from Ethiopia we call carbuncle.

It sounds like something out of Ryder Haggard's *King Solomon's Mines*, or an Indiana Jones adventure. However, when one reads Herodotus, who lived over 400 years before Pliny, there is the story about the salt-house dwellers but with a little more detail; Herodotus says:

> As far as the Atlantes the names of the nations inhabiting the sandy ridge are known to me; but beyond them my knowledge fails. The ridge itself extends as far as the pillars of Hercules [Gibraltar straits], and even further than these and throughout the whole distance, at the end of every ten days journey there is a salt mine, with people dwelling round it who all of them build their houses with blocks of salt. No rain falls in these parts of Libya [Africa] if it were otherwise the walls of the houses

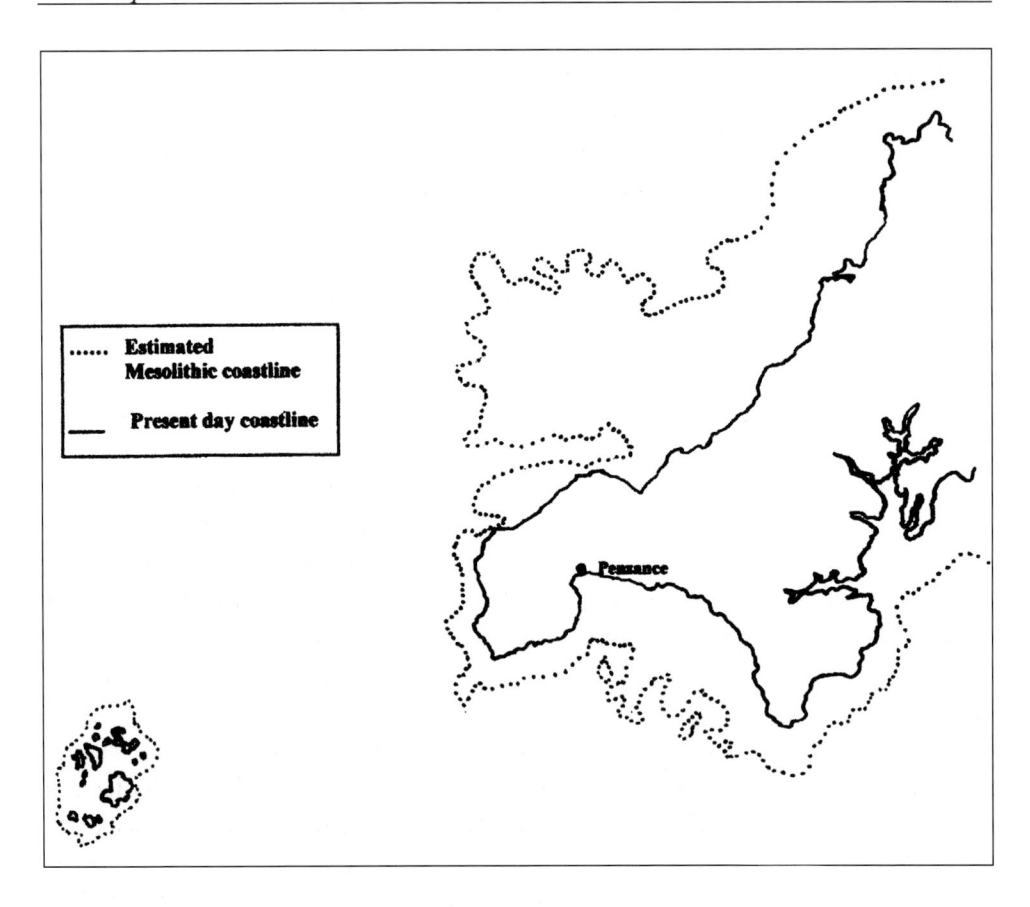

1 An estimate of the coastline during the Mesolithic around Mounts Bay and the Isles of Scilly showing where the lost land of Lyonesse could have been

could not stand. The salt quarried is of two colours, white and purple. Beyond the ridge southwards in the direction of the interior the country is a desert, with no springs, no beasts, no rain, no wood and altogether devoid of moisture.

If Pliny read Herodotus to get this information, this work would have already been 400 years old. It is fascinating to think of Pliny reading an ancient book and adding information from it to his own history book, which itself is now 2000 years old. It does show, however, that people adapt to their environment and can live in areas that no one would choose to inhabit, although the circumstances that led them to live in such a desperate place were probably unknown to either Pliny or Herodotus. Why did these people not dwell in a more fertile region? Their tribal legends would probably explain the origins for these salt miners living in houses made of blocks of salt if only Herodotus had thought to ask.

Prehistory in Britain is the time before the Roman conquest. The people who lived in the British Isles were like the bushmen of the Kalahari today — with a verbal, not a written culture — who passed down knowledge from generation to generation in the form of stories and legends. Even today, we can still decipher these legends and find a seed of truth in them from their prehistoric origins. In Cornwall, there is a good example of this sort of link to our distant past through a legend in the Penzance area which states that there was once a land called Lyonesse far off the coast of present-day Mounts Bay.

The story goes that Trevelyan, the king of Lyonesse, was the only person to escape the flood when the sea engulfed the land. Seeing the advancing waters, he quickly leapt onto the back of a fast white horse and reached a high rock in the dense forest. There, hiding in a cave, he watched the disaster sweep over Lyonesse, until only the hilltops were left above the waves. Trevelyan was so grateful to his high refuge for saving him that he dedicated it to God as a spiritual place for all time. Legend has it that this rock in the forest is now St Michael's Mount and the hilltops of vanished Lyonesse are the Isles of Scilly.

The truth of part of this legend can be seen during very low tides, or after a storm at sea. At the edge of the shoreline can be found petrified wood, that is, wood turned to stone over thousands of years (**1**). Geologists believe that the sea level in the Mesolithic was about 34m lower that it is today. If one looks at a nautical map of Mounts Bay and one traces the 34m depth you can see a vast plain that is now the modern bay. So here you can see part of the rich forest of Lyonesse, now submerged. The shoreline of this rich forest would have been inhabited by hunter-gatherer tribes. When the ice began to melt at the end of the last glacial period, these low-lying areas were submerged by the rising waters.

Let us imagine how life changed for the people that lived on this land before it was submerged and became either the English Channel or the North Sea. Each year, the rivers they crossed on their hunting expeditions would have become wider and deeper. Lakes would begin to be formed and the land around the lakes would become a spongy marshland. Their normal pathways would have to alter, perhaps each year, to take account of newly waterlogged land. Safe, dry campsites would perhaps have been further away from traditional hunting grounds, so the people would eventually abandon the wetlands and move to the higher ground. They then became a shoreline culture — choosing to settle in either Britain if they were the people of Lyonesse or, if their lands were under our present-day North Sea, either in Denmark, or along the shoreline of the east coast of Britain.

Apart from these legendary glimpses of past realities, the only way to open the door into our prehistoric past is from the archaeological record. The earliest finds are flint, antler and bone which have been shaped into tools. These are the day-to-day objects for the hunter-gatherer, just as they are for prehistoric societies today, such as the bushmen, Amazonian Indians and Inuit peoples of North America. We know this because, when one looks at the tools and day-to-day equipment of these primitive people, they are almost identical to the tools found in the archaeological record.

2 The hunter-gatherers

To understand the lives and food of the European hunter-gatherers, it is important to imagine the type of landscape they lived in — the Europe they knew was a very different place to the one we know today. At the time of the early Mesolithic period (or middle Stone Age, roughly 12,000 BC), it would have been possible to walk from the east coast of Britain to Denmark and south to the rest of Europe (**2**). The land between modern-day Britain and Denmark was known as Doggerland and, as the ice sheets began to melt, the north coast of this region shifted southward, causing the high central mountains to become an island (**3**) about 6700 BC. The people who lived in these Dogger hills thus became islanders who, for approximately 400 years, occupied a slowly shrinking land of large estuaries, lagoons and forests.

Up until this time, Britain had been joined to continental Europe by a narrow land bridge which, along with Dogger Island, was finally submerged in about 6300 BC, thereby turning Britain into an island. It is assumed that the remaining population travelled in log boats to the east coast of Britain which was their nearest land mass. All that is left of the ancient mountains of Doggerland are the shallow waters of what is now the Dogger Bank, a fishing area in the North Sea. Even today, trawlers that fish these waters occasionally bring up antlers, bones and the roots of trees from the top of this 150-mile long sandbank.

Before the ice sheets melted, a hunter and his family could, in time, have slowly hunted their way from Russia to the west coast of Britain. Along their way, they would have found very much the same kinds of wild vegetation and forests (**4**). In the north of Britain, there is archaeological evidence for people living at a spring base-camp at a famous site called Star Carr in north Yorkshire. It is thought that their temporary dwellings were scooped-out hollows in the ground, but there is little evidence for this assumption. Their dwellings were more probably some sort of tent-like structure, covered with animal skins like the American plains Indians used. There is also the possibility that their dwellings were wooden frames covered with the water reeds which would have surrounded this ancient lakeside. Various artefacts have been found at Star Carr, such as wooden and bone fishing harpoons, and a wooden paddle. This suggests that they probably had dug-out canoes, although none have been found to date. Not only were the bones of their prey excavated, but also the bones of their dogs that were probably used for hunting.

2 An estimate of the coastline approx. 10,000 years ago. The dots indicate the modern coastline

One of the most famous finds from this site is a set of antlers, with holes perforated in the front of them so that they could be tied onto someone's head. This could have been a useful tool when approaching a herd of deer when hunting, but has been relegated by most archaeologists to having some ritualistic significance — such as part of a ritual dance to a deer god. It is often the case with academic archaeologists that, when in doubt as to the function of a particular artefact, it is thought that it must be ritualistic.

There has been some new research in recent years looking at the connection between beavers and Mesolithic cultures. When sticks from this site were examined in detail, it was found that quite a high proportion of them had beaver teeth marks on them, showing that they had been felled by beavers. If I were a Mesolithic hunter, I would definitely search out areas of beaver habitation when

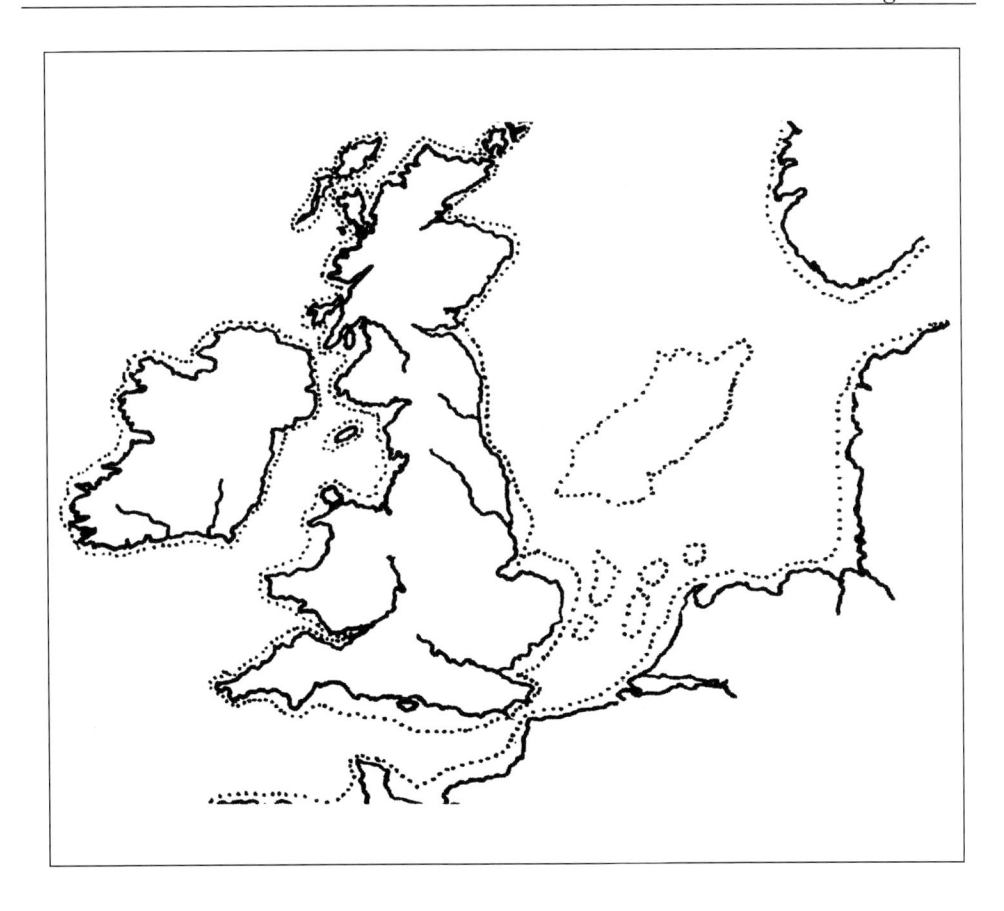

3 An estimate of the coastline approx. 8,400 years ago showing the Dogger Island before it was covered by glacial waters. The dots indicate the modern coastline

I decided to make a camp. When walking in a beaver-occupied forest in Poland, I was amazed at the number of trees felled by these little creatures; it was like a logging camp. The beavers only use the branches of the trees to make their lodges and dams in the rivers, so the main trunks of the trees were trimmed and left. Every so often, there was an example of what my Polish guide called 'beaver art' (**5**), that is, trees that had been double-cut by a beaver for some reason and left as a testimony to its indecisiveness. So if a hunter and his family lived near a beaver dam, they would have a ready supply of felled timber, an artificial lake to fish in which would attract forest game, and beavers themselves for meat and fur.

Not far away from Star Carr, at Poulton Le Fyde in Lancashire, there is a wonderful reconstruction made by archaeologists from the site evidence. From the silted-up bed of a prehistoric pool, they recovered the complete skeleton of an elk with bone harpoon heads embedded in it dating to approximately 9000 BC. The environmental archaeologists analysed the pollen evidence and found that

4 The density of Mesolithic forests

5 A picture of what is known in Poland as beaver art. It is a common sight in beaver felled forests, which would have been good environments in which to set up Mesolithic camps

birch trees had surrounded this pond and, due to the condition of the elk's antlers, it must have been winter when it died. After careful study of the animal's bones it was thought that the animal was about six years old and had been attacked and wounded over a period of nine or ten days. Some of the wounds had been made by flint-tipped arrows and others by axes. Piecing together all this information, the archaeologists painted a graphic picture of a possible scene beside this ancient pond in the winter of 11,000 years ago. A group of hunters had probably hunted this particular animal over nine to ten days, gradually weakening it with chance shots from their arrows and axes. In a vain attempt to escape, the wounded animal had run across the ice of a small frozen lake. The ice was too thin, and the animal had sunk into the icy waters of the lake, well beyond the abilities of the hunters to retrieve it. So a disappointing week's hunting for a band of Mesolithic people provides us with a unique insight into a moment from another time.

It was not just the landscape that was changing at this time; the type of game also began to change. Reindeer became less common as herds of deer, elk, wild cattle and boar moved north due to the change in vegetation. The tundra vegetation gave way to lush grasses and plants such as gentians, saxifrages, meadowsweet and dock; all of which have been found in the pollen record for this

6 An example of a primitive trackway made to cross marshland. The whole construction is made from scrub willow

period by environmental archaeologists. This vegetation then began to be colonised by shrubs such as juniper, willow, birch and finally hazel. Hazel scrub subsequently became a dominant feature in the landscape until the first trees started to colonise this newly fertile region. These trees, predominantly pine, oak, elm and ash, started to overshadow the hazel scrub until, in the course of a handful of generations, the land became dense, rich forest. In this new landscape, the only open features were lakes and bog-land. Reed swamp gradually developed (**colour plate 1**) and was eventually replaced by raised bog in areas where sphagnum or bog mosses predominated.

Through this rich and fertile land vast herds of deer and wild cattle would roam. These herds wandering through the landscape, following the contours and ridges of the land, produced route ways to watering holes that the hunter could follow. These people seemed to travel for part of the year and spend their summers in temporary camps by the shoreline of either lake or sea, with the game route ways leading them through the dense forest to these transient camps. Some of these ancient route ways became our existing roads and trackways today — some 12-14,000 years of almost constant use (**6**).

Let us look across the land of Dogger to another tribe in what is now southern Scandinavia. Due to the development of marine archaeology, we can see how hunter-gatherer tribes inhabited land near a submerged riverbed. Excavations began in 1979 at the bottom of Oresund Strait, following the course of the submerged river Saxan. From a study of nautical charts, it was possible to trace the course of the river and any raised shoreline that might have been inhabited. Three early Mesolithic settlements were found 6-20m below sea level. A subsequent excavation in 1995 revealed flint artefacts as well as the bones of roe deer, red deer, aurochs, and the remains of burnt sticks from a fire. Somehow the burnt sticks and animal bones really capture the imagination; someone thousands of years ago sitting by a campfire on the river bank, eating spit-roasted venison or roast beef. Now ships sail 20m above this place in the straits between Denmark and Sweden.

Across the straits in Denmark lies the most thoroughly investigated Mesolithic culture in northern Europe, the Ertebolle Culture. Tybrind Vig was the first archaeological site to be excavated underwater in Denmark. It was discovered by amateur divers in 1978 and lies some 250m from a present-day beach in western Flyn. A trial investigation uncovered undisturbed layers containing artefacts, animal bones, antlers, leaves, fruits, seeds, and tree trunks. A shallow pit in this submerged site revealed the body of a girl, 15-17 years old with a newborn baby laid across her chest. There was no indication as to the cause of death, although it might possibly have been during childbirth. A later analysis of her bones revealed that her diet was mainly composed of fish, shellfish and seal. These people lived by hunting, fishing and gathering — as many of the artefacts found show us. Their middens were not just full of the bones of edible animals, but also those that

7 The first artist impression of the Tybrind Vig boat, here being used at night to catch eels. A fire is made on stones at one end of the boat and one of the fishermen is holding a flare over the water to attract the eels. The other is waiting with a harpoon to spear them

must have been primarily hunted for their furs — fox, wildcat, otter, badger and pine marten. There are even clearly visible flint cuts on the skulls of these animals, probably caused during skinning. The remains of hazelnuts, acorns and seashells also give us an insight to the variety of their diet.

The large quantity of fishing equipment, including fishing nets, showed that they must have had some form of vessel with which to fish offshore. It was hoped that this vessel might be found and eventually it was — in fact, it was the first whole boat found in a Mesolithic Danish settlement context. The boat was made out of a straight-trunked lime tree and from the wood analysis it was found to have been made with axes and adzes. The Tybrind boat, as it is called, was 9.5m long, 0.65m wide and 3cm thick. A large stone weighing 30kg was found in the boat, probably put there as ballast. It was a uniform trough shape, 30cm high, and was smooth and rounded on the outside. Along with this canoe were found ten different kinds of paddle made of ash wood. Two of the bigger ones are elaborately decorated and are the first decorated Mesolithic wood to be found in Europe. An oval fireplace of sand and small stones was found 0.5m inside the stern of the boat.

This feature is characteristic of many Stone Age Danish boats and is probably connected with eel fishing. To do this, flares were made from burning sticks to attract the fish to the boat at night (**7**). Yet it is also a pleasant thought to imagine a couple of fishermen — maybe father and son — out in the bay on a still autumn evening with a little fire to catch and cook the fish they had caught, and to keep warm by. Somehow, pieces of archaeology like this bridge the gap between our time and a long distant past. It shows us that people have not really changed very much; life was still about providing food and keeping warm on a cold night.

Small fragments of textiles were also found on the site, spun out of some type of vegetable fibre — possibly nettle — but scientific analysis is still pending on this find. These textiles are the first found from the European Mesolithic period and give us more insight into Mesolithic society. This period was so long ago that finds such as these have only just come to light because of modern archaeological methods of excavation. Up to now, we did not think that any textiles were produced in this period mainly because we had not found any. Some archaeologists can have a very narrow perception of the hunter-gatherer cultures of the past. It is assumed that 'if we have not found a particular object, then it must not have existed', ignoring the fact that these people would probably have needed some form of textile, or rope, or fishing net in their daily lives. So I would rather assume that they *did* have some textiles and wait until archaeology turns them up one day. I prefer to give the benefit of the doubt to the ingenuity of the prehistoric people and feel that they were quite capable of accomplishing a great deal more than we give them credit for.

Somehow, because *ancient* hunter-gatherers are so distant from our modern-day European society, we disconnect them totally from *current* prehistoric cultures. It is wholly acceptable that Amazonian Indians understand the uses, medical and culinary, of all the vegetation near their forest homes. When one looks at a prehistoric site, a comprehensive pollen analysis will inform us what vegetation was growing in the area. Yet unless residues of these plants are actually found in vessels, it is sometimes assumed that our forbears did not use them.

However, if it was available and tasted good, it would have been consumed. Apart from the climate, why should our prehistoric forbears' lives have been any different from the forest-dwellers of the Amazon today?

3 The first farmers

The first farmers of northern Europe are known to have cultivated the land thousands of years later than the people of Eurasia. The earliest archaeological evidence to date is from Jericho where the remains of organised settlements and domesticated crops have been found. These crops were of barley, einkorn and emmer wheat, and pulses such as lentil, peas and chickpeas. Flax has also been found from this period dating from approximately 9000 years ago, which suggests that linseed was used for food and linen for cloth. At Nahal Hemar, a contemporary cave site near Galilee, textiles and nets have been discovered made of fine linen thread. By about 8000 years ago Neolithic agriculture occured widely from Iran to western Turkey and domesticated goats and sheep also appear in these regions for the first time at sites in the Taurus and Zagros Mountains. Yet it appears from the archaeology that the first farmers in the north started growing crops around 4000 BC, nearly 3000 years later than in the middle east. In recent years, it has been a great topic of debate as to why the hunter-gatherers would want to leave their established way of life for the drudgery of crop farming. In a recent article in *British Archaeology,* Dr Peter Rowley-Conwy of Durham University states

> Archaeologists have traditionally placed hunter-gatherers at the bottom of the social evolutionary heap. Some have given the impression that the most interesting thing about hunter-gatherers is that they finally gave it up and started farming . . . But contrary to popular belief, agriculture is not an inevitable advance. We call hard but boring work 'the daily grind' a reference to milling cultivated grain, and current research is showing that you didn't take up farming unless you had to.

If this is the case, why did the hunter-gatherers of northern Europe decide to settle, and become farmers? One school of thought in Denmark is that the population grew to such an extent, that there were just too many people relying on ever decreasing herds of game. The fact remains that the cultural pattern of the Ertebolle people undergoes a profound change about 4000 BC. Their hunter-fisher culture suddenly disappears and, over a short time-span, archaeologists find entirely new types of settlements, daily objects, dwellings and religious artefacts.

The first farmers

8 An artistic impression to demonstrate what it might have been like for a couple of Mesolithic hunters to arrive at a well-known hunting forest to find all the Elm trees had died and a green swath of grass land stretched into the distance. It must have been a strange sight to a people that were used to dense forest: the only open spaces they knew were stretches of water

This apparent sudden change in the archaeological record is found throughout the north during this period. It is possible that more than one force drove these people to change a way of life that had sustained them for many thousands of years. This might have been because the forest landscape that they lived in suddenly changed. Environmental archaeologists have long known that 30 per cent of the dense forests that covered northern Europe were made up of elm trees. They know this from the percentage of elm spores in pollen analysis in the prehistoric levels. It is due to the sudden disappearance of all of the elm pollen that archaeologists formed the assumption that the first farmers had appeared. The reason for this is that these farmers must have cut down all the elm trees to make clearings in the dense forest to grow the first crops. No one thought to question this assumption until in the 1970s when Dutch Elm disease swept over Europe and decimated the elm population due to the activity of the Dutch Elm beetle. Archaeologists started to wonder if this was the first time that this had happened in European history. It was not until the late 1980s that an environmental archaeologist studying samples for a site at West Spa in Hampstead

9 An artistic impression of an Iron Age lake dwelling

found the remains of elm beetles in deposits predating the decline in elm pollen around 4000 BC. The hunter-gatherers perhaps found that large tracts of the forest had died (**8**) and forest clearings appeared at the same time as the game they hunted became more scarce. It might have been a combination of these factors which encouraged them to change their way of life. The climate at this time is thought to have been mainly warm summers and mild winters, and crop growing would have been an easy skill to acquire in such favourable conditions. The land would also have been incredibly fertile for the first few years, due to the forest nutrients; just as the rainforests are fertile when the forests are cut down today.

In Europe the most famous Neolithic settlements tend to be found on the edge of lakes (**colour plate 2**). In Switzerland in the eighteenth century, Ferdinand Keller discovered an accumulation of stakes in Lake Zurich that he believed came from the remains of prehistoric dwellings. He believed them to be possible lake dwellings, similar to those mentioned in the fourth century BC by Herodotus who described a settlement close to Macedonia, giving us a wonderful insight into the daily lives of such lake dwellers:

> The houses of these lake dwellers are actually in the water and stand on platforms supported on long piles and approached from the land by a

single narrow bridge. Originally the labour of driving the piles was presumably undertaken by the tribe as a whole, but later they adopted a different method; now the piles are brought from Mt. Orbelus and every man drives in three for each wife he marries and each has a great many wives. Each member of the tribe has his own hut on one of the platforms, with a trap-door opening on to the water underneath. To prevent their babies from tumbling in, they tie a string to their legs. Their horses and other pack animals they feed on fish, which are so abundant in the lake, that when they open the trap door and let down an empty basket on a rope, they have only a minute to wait before they pull it up again, full. (9)

In Switzerland they started to look for more evidence of lake dwellings and moorland settlements in the dried-up alpine lake areas — they found another 100 sites, then 200. Tens of thousands of finds were collected, mostly stone axes and flint, but also wood, woven fabric and metal finds from a later period, all in excellent condition, which were then distributed to various museums in the area. It was not until the 1920s that a more scientific excavation was undertaken on Lake Constance and more detailed information was revealed to the archaeological world. This led to the building of the first open-air museum in Europe. The archaeologists, fuelled with a wealth of details excavated from this wetland site began making exact, life-sized reconstructions of the finds between 1922 and 1940, and up to the present day. The aim of this centre at Unteruhldingen was to present a graphic and lively representation of everyday life in a lake dwelling in the Stone Age. This centre is still thriving with different types of reconstructed dwellings from different periods of the lake's history. There are many sites like this found throughout Europe, yet one of the most thoroughly excavated is in Britain at the Glastonbury lake village in Somerset. Although these are from the later Iron Age period, the principle is the same in that these people lived in houses built on stilts at the edge of a lake. Although the initial building would have been more labour-intensive than building a house on land, it definitely had its advantages. One could sleep peacefully in one's bed at night, as no wild animal could get into your house and attack you. Also, your water supply was very convenient to you: just open the trap door, and lower down a bucket. If Herodotus was right, you would possibly pull up a bucket full of fish with the water. Waterfowl would live in your vicinity, and the reeds to thatch your houses would grow around the lake edge. In the spring, there would be a ready supply of duck eggs to be gathered from the lake edge in the lush vegetation which could also be harvested. Land around lakes tends to be very rich and silt-laden, so growing your first crops would be easier than trying to break up stony soils farther inland.

Due to the waterlogged condition of this Swiss lake site, wonderful evidence was found which showed many aspects of daily life in the Stone Age. Different kinds of grains such as einkorn and emmer wheat's, barley, peas, lentils, poppy and flax were found. A wild harvest of crab apple, sloe, haw, beech nuts, acorns, hazelnuts and berries was discovered in the Stone Age layers of the silts. There were bones of domesticated cattle, sheep (see **colour plate 14**) and goats, as well as the wide variety of game still available to these first farmers. The Stone Age farmers experimented with the beginnings of pottery production and there were even examples of pottery repairs being made. A lake villager had glued a broken pot with some birch bark tar to make it useable. This tar was distilled in underground pots from the fine bark of the birch tree; it is also said by modern herbalists to have pain-killing properties. At one of the sites, a piece of bark tar was found with human teeth marks in it, so some archaeologists think it may have been the forerunner of chewing-gum. At a site in Sweden called Bokeberg, dated to 4500 BC, a piece of chewed tar has been found with the teeth impressions of a 30- to 40-year-old person, showing a cavity in one tooth. Maybe the bark was chewed and then stuck into a cavity, as a crude form of dentistry — as long as people have had teeth, there have been cavities and toothache.

Pottery production in the Neolithic period was very simple, yet in the later part of the Danish Neolithic the pots achieve great artistic heights and have particularly detailed ornamentation that is unsurpassed in later Danish prehistory. The pots were probably fired in an open fire and made with local clay sources.

In the past few years, there have been numerous discoveries of Neolithic dwellings in Britain and Europe, although the most famous is still Skara Brae in the Orkneys which was discovered in 1850 after a severe storm blew away the sand that covered this shore-line village. The village consists of nine huts made out of dry-stone walling which were probably roofed with turf or thatch. All the dwellings are linked together with lined stone passageways. The most remarkable feature of this village is the stone furniture. In one of the houses, a stone bed made of slate slabs was set on each side of the hearth and stone shelving was made against a wall with small stone pillars supporting the shelves. Their food remains were found in the midden, as well as pestles, pottery shards, adzes, mortars and axes. Neolithic people also worked out how to make pottery because, in their more settled existence, they needed containers not just to cook with, but also to store grains and liquids. There is even evidence from residues in a pot from Skara Brae that some form of beer was brewed using a herb called meadowsweet. Brewing tests have shown that the addition of meadowsweet extends the shelf-life of beer made in a primitive manner by many weeks.

One of the great mysteries for archaeologists in Britain who study the Neolithic period is the lack of evidence for the cultivation of crops. Such evidence is abundant in European sites with many finds of primitive wheat and barley grains. Although some Neolithic dwellings have been found in Britain, there have been almost no finds of field systems from this period. This has led to research by archaeologists to ascertain why Britain lagged behind the rest of Europe in the cultivation of crops. Recent researches by Mike Richards, a Ph.D. student at the research laboratory for archaeology in Oxford, states:

> The small-scale study, the first of its kind, of the bones of about 23 Neolithic people from ten sites in central and southern England, suggests that these first farmers relied heavily on animal meat for food, or on animal by-products such as milk and cheese, and that plant foods in fact, formed little importance in their diet.

A comparative study of Iron Age people who were known to have grown cereal was very different. Animal remains in Neolithic Britain are generally those of domestic cattle and pigs. So it appears that the first settlers in Britain were stockmen and did not find the need to grow crops until much later in the Bronze Age period when evidence of grains and field systems is common. There is another quotation from Herodotus, about an Ethiopian king talking to a Persian emissary in the fourth century BC. He had some very strong views about people that grew grain, as you will see; maybe the Neolithic people in Britain felt the same. We will probably never know but it is interesting to surmise. Here is the quotation:

> . . . he asked what the Persian king ate and what was the greatest age that Persians could attain. Getting in reply an account of the nature and cultivation of wheat, and hearing that people in Persia did not commonly live beyond eighty. He said that he was not surprised that anyone who ate dung should die so soon . . . in their turn, the Persians asked the king how long the Ethiopians lived and what they ate, and were told that most of them lived to be a hundred and twenty and some even more and that they ate boiled meat and drank milk

He obviously thought that as the wheat was grown with manure, that manure is what they were eating in a different form.

So the first farmers began their labours in different parts of Europe at different times. By the time metals such as copper and then bronze became a part of European culture, the crops and farming methods throughout Europe were very much the same.

4 The first metals: the Bronze Age

Copper

The system of describing the ages of humanity by three definite periods — the *Stone Age*, *Bronze Age* and *Iron Age* — was invented in Denmark in 1836, mainly to classify museum collections. Modern archaeology finds this simplistic approach a little dated as nothing in man's evolution is so cut-and-dried — the ages did not start and finish uniformly when a new tool medium arrived. The transition between different materials would have been gradual and possibly erratic, depending on a culture's desire to change the *status quo*. It is this time of transition which is becoming increasingly popular with modern-day researchers in their desire to undermine these previously immovable benchmarks. The term 'Bronze Age' is the term used for the period when the first metals were used, and not when the first bronze alloy was made; the beginning of the Bronze Age occurred when copper was first smelted and fashioned into useful objects. The discovery of the Ice Man (**10**) on the Austrian-Italian border in 1991 was to throw conventional time spans for these ages in Europe into complete confusion. The Neolithic period or 'first farmers' period in Europe was thought to last up to approximately 2200 BC — in other words, no culture was thought to have metals in northern Europe until just after this date, the beginning of the Bronze Age. The discovery of the Ice Man, and his subsequent dating to 3300 BC, with a fine copper axe in his possession, took the archaeological world by storm. This find proves that the date for the beginning of the Bronze Age and the use of metals must now be pushed back over 1000 years; which is why this particular find has engendered such intense academic interest.

The dating of finds and their attribution to particular cultures has, from Neolithic times, revolved around the pottery they produced. Each culture seems to produce a particular type of pottery, or perhaps a particular type of pottery decoration. Archaeologists are so confident with this method of classification of peoples throughout the prehistoric period that they actually name the culture by the type of pottery they produce. In the alpine region, close to where the Ice Man was found, there is a culture called the 'square-mouthed pot culture'. One wonders what these societies would think if they knew they were classified by something that they probably thought was of little importance to them, such as

The first metals: the Bronze Age

10 The 'Ice Man' reconstruction in the Museum of the South Tyrol in Bolzano, Northern Italy. The model is wearing the grass cloak and shoes that I made for the museum

the shape of their cooking pots. It is the same as calling the people of Staffordshire the 'willow pattern culture' because they made so much of it. Basically pottery does not decay over millennia spent in the ground, so it tends to be the most common find at archaeological excavations, hence this pottery-naming practice. If the Ice Man had had a piece of pottery with him, it might have been relatively easy to find which area he came from. Of course, he could have come from a culture not yet discovered. This particular alpine region where he was found is notorious for landslides and avalanches. If a narrow ravine is blocked by a landslide, a stream course could be diverted or blocked and a lake formed. Underneath an undulating pattern of scree and stream re-routing, it is easy to imagine that many alpine cultures became lost. The region is also inaccessible most of the year due to snowfalls. It is tantalising to think of just what could be found if a systematic survey of the alpine regions were ever undertaken. I have a personal interest in the Ice Man find because I had been researching the possible prehistoric uses of moorland grasses for a number of years before the Ice Man's discovery. I noticed in Conrad Spindler's book about him that some of the plaiting techniques on his grass cloak were almost identical to techniques devised in my research. This led to me acquiring more detailed information of the finds and reconstructing his shoes and grass cloak over the last few years. Due to this research, I was commissioned to make the reconstructions of his shoes and grass cloak for the museum to be dedicated to him at Bolzano, in northern Italy.

At copper age sites in Europe, there was a distinctive type of pottery called Beaker; it was made of thin red pottery and S-shaped in profile, and was highly decorated with elaborate geometric patterns. This Beaker pottery is found during the period around 2550 BC in very distant parts of Europe, from the highlands of Scotland to the south of modern-day Portugal, from Germany to Hungary and to the west coast of France (**colour plates 3 & 4**).

The way that the Beaker people buried their dead was also distinctive. Whereas the Neolithic peoples tended to have collective burial chamber tombs and round barrows, the Beaker folk tended to be buried in a crouched position, individually, in a pit or stone cist (a coffin made with large stone slabs) with a bell-shaped Beaker pot. A study of Beaker burials in Yorkshire showed that most men were buried facing east, to the sun and females facing west, to the moon. The average Beaker package of grave goods tends to be arrowheads, wrist-guards, daggers and axes, also some gold ornamentation. The sudden appearance of these Beaker pots, metal items and different burial practices has created many theories as to who these people were. Were they just traders, bringing metal technology in their wake and new religious concepts — hence the different burials — or were they some sort of colonists or invaders? No one knows, but various residues found in these Beaker pots have lead to some theories. At Ashgrove in Scotland, a pot was found to contain meadowsweet and a lot of lime pollen; lime pollen is known not to have grown north of Cumbria. So the contents must have been made in the south and brought to Scotland, possibly inside the vessel. Some archaeologists think that the residue is the remains of a lime/mead drink. It has even been suggested by some that the Beaker people, in addition to their knowledge of metalworking, were also traders of some sort of alcoholic drink, packaged in the distinctive Beaker shaped pots and maybe sealed with a wooden stopper. This is total conjecture, although it is interesting that the Beaker pots were so widely distributed and that the source of the lime pollen was outside the region in Scotland where the pot was found.

However, the earliest known copper mine for the Beaker culture in north-western Europe was on Ross Island, County Kerry, in Ireland. The discovery of early Beaker pottery at the work camp of this mine is firmly associated with mine residues dating from 2400-2000 BC, confirming the time it was used for metal ore extraction. Archaeologists think that these small pottery vessels were used as drinking cups by the miners. Another typical object found in connection with this beaker culture is the gold lunulae (**colour plate 5**) or crescent-shaped neckpiece made out of beaten gold. These have been found not only in Ireland, but in southern Scotland and Cornwall. In burials in Yorkshire, jet beads have been found and in Dorset shale, a type of black slate was fashioned into bracelets for the Beaker people.

Bronze

The making of bronze was the next development of metallurgy in Europe. A proportion of one part tin to nine parts copper made a metal far harder and more durable than copper alone. The sources of the tin ore to produce this higher-quality metal were scarce, especially when its usefulness became known. The main areas in which tin was found in Europe were Bohemia, and Cornwall in the south-west of Britain. Diodorus Siculus, the Sicilian historian wrote in AD 60 about the ancient Cornish tin trade with Europe:

> They that inhabit the British promontory of Belarium [west Cornwall] by reason of their converse with merchants, are more courteous to strangers than the rest. These are the people that make the tin, which with a great deal of care and labour they dig out of the ground; and being rocky, the metal is mixed with some veins of earth, out of which they melt the metal and refine it: Then they beat it into four square pieces like a die, and carry it to a British Isle near at hand, called Ictis [St Michael's Mount] (**colour plate 6**). For at low tide all being dry between them and the island, they convey over carts abundance of tin

in the mean time . . . Hence the merchants transport the tin they buy off the inhabitants to France; and for 30 days journey, they carry it in packs on horses backs through France to the river Rhodanus [Rhône].

There is an account by another classical historian, Strabo, who writes about how jealously guarded the Cassiderides' (Tin Isles) location was:

[They]. . . are inhabited by people who wear black cloaks, go clad in tunics that reach to their feet, wear belts around their breasts, walk with canes and resemble the goddesses of vengeance in tragedies . . . As they have mines of tin and lead, they give these metals and the hides from their cattle to the sea traders in exchange for pottery, salt and copper utensils. Now in former times it was the Phoenicians alone, who carried on this commerce for they kept the voyage hidden from every one else. And when once the Romans were closely following a certain ship captain, in order that they too might learn the markets in question; out of jealousy the ship captain purposely drove his ship out of its course into shallow water; and after he had lured the followers into the same ruin, he himself escaped by a piece of wreckage and received from the state the value of the cargo he had lost.

So with an increasing demand for the new harder metal, tin sources were indeed a precious commodity — these trade routes are considered in more detail in the chapter on the Iron Age. Of course, copper was also required in nine times the quantity of tin in order to make bronze, so large copper-mining developments have also been discovered from the period. It is estimated that 32 shafts were dug in the Austrian Alps at Mitterberg, which were thought to have possibly produced 10,000 metric tons of crude copper. The Bronze Age people of Europe would have required a complex system of trade routes to carry raw materials to smelting centres and manufacturing sites and it is known from archaeological finds that manufactured goods were distributed throughout the entire region. Hungarian swords have been found in Denmark, and Breton axes are found in Switzerland. In their desire for bronze, people had to develop tradeable commodities in order to purchase either the manufactured goods or ores for smelting. These commodities were as varied as furs, slaves, gold, amber and delicate faience (an early form of glass) beads; the lists of trade goods are endless. Of course, in order to move these ever increasing quantities and types of goods, better methods of transportation had to be developed. As Strabo said of the later period, packhorses were used to transport tin to the Mediterranean after crossing the Channel and there is archaeological evidence of wheeled transports being developed at this time, with horses and oxen being used to pull wagons and carts. However, the

11 A typical log Boat used not just in the Mesolithic but up to medieval times for river trade in Europe

trackways used were probably the remains of the ancient route ways of the hunter-gatherer period. These would be passable in the summer months but would have become impassable for heavy wagons during wet weather. So other, more reliable means of transport were required, such as boats (**11**).

As mentioned earlier, dugout canoes have been found throughout Europe (**colour plate 7**). On a 4km stretch of the River Brivet (a tributary of the Loire), 40-50 dugout canoes dating from Neolithic times to as late as AD 1025 were excavated in 1994. In 1974, on the seabed near Dover, part of the cargo of a boat, mainly broken metalwork dating from the Bronze Age, was discovered, proving the existence of cross channel trade at this time. Yet one of the most spectacular boat finds from the Bronze Age period was in 1992 at Dover again. This was an almost complete vessel about one and a half times the length of a double-decker bus. In an article in *British Archaeology* in May 1997, Peter Clarke, the director of the trust funded to reconstruct a copy of this boat, describes this wonderful vessel in detail.

> The boat (tentatively dated to around 1300 BC in the middle Bronze Age) consists, in essence, of four oak planks: two flat bottom planks and two curved side planks — although additional side planks had been

removed in antiquity. The bottom planks were fixed together without nails or carpentry joints, but by ramming wedges and cross-timbers through a pair of upstanding ridges on either side of the main joint and through a series of cleats (or semi-circular wooden hoops). This technique seems strange, as the main joint appears to be a line of weakness where we would expect a strong keel. We know from other Bronze Age boats that carpentry jointing was known at the time, but for some reason it was not used . . . The sheer scale of the boat suggests that it was a sea-going vessel, though this question is still hotly disputed.

There are still some who do not believe that cross-channel trade occurred at this time. The members of this school of thought are dwindling rapidly, however, due to finds such as these. There are traces of grooves on the bottom of the boat, which suggests that it was beached rather than moored in a harbour. At the bottom of the boat was found a scrap of unworked shale from Kimmeridge Bay in Dorset; this particular shale was known to have been fashioned into various items of trade in the Bronze Age, such as beads, belt rings, pendants and rings, some of which were covered with gold. A bowl in the shape of a boat, made of shale and inlaid with gold, was excavated in Wales.

As the population grew, so there was more pressure on the land to support it. The decline in fertility of over-farmed Neolithic fields required more of the marginal uplands, such as moorland areas, to be cultivated. Field boundaries became important as land, and what it produced, had a market value with the non-farming metallurgical communities. Animal bones in middens show a reduction in species that were hunted as it became more profitable to rear livestock in corrals on farms, rather than to spend days hunting animals in the ever decreasing forests of Europe. Axes of bronze begin to be found in the archaeological record and curved bronze sickles replace the straight wooden sickles with flint blades. The introduction of the ard, or primitive plough, was also common — using the already-domesticated horses and oxen to pull it. There is a variety of evidence for a uniformly popular ploughshare being used, illustrated in various rock art of the time. There also was a uniformity in the type of dwellings that these farming communities lived in. The average houses were made of either stone, or wattle and daub, depending on which building material was abundant in the area. The shape of these dwellings tended to be roughly rectangular, or maybe a long oval shape. Yet during the time of the first metals in Britain, the previously rectangular or oval Neolithic dwellings suddenly become round; the British roundhouse was born (**colour plate 8**). No one knows why this should be; it is just the case that archaeologists find roundhouses in Britain from the Bronze Age right up to the Saxon period, whilst the rest of Europe retains the rectangular shape.

The first metals: the Bronze Age

12 A sprang frame, demonstrating the Bronze Age twisted thread technique

There is an even more interesting phenomenon: in roundhouse villages there is often one square house whereas, at some village sites in Europe, there is evidence for one house being round; why this should be is totally unknown. I have my own theory which, I might add, is total conjecture. Maybe the roundhouse in the European village was the house of a chief or priest and a very special place to dwell in. Maybe the first metal-workers who crossed the channel at the end of the Neolithic period decided to settle; perhaps they had always liked the roundhouses in their European villages but were unable to live in them due to some strict social convention. In this new land they could overturn convention and *all* live in roundhouses if they chose. So that they could differentiate between ordinary houses and that of the chief or priest, they built one square one for that purpose. Until archaeology comes up with a better idea, this is as good a theory as any.

Within these villages, most of the requirements of daily life would have been met by the community, textile production being but one of the many crafts needed by these people. Unfortunately, textiles do not survive well over 3500 years unless the conditions in which they are found are favourable to their preservation. One such place is in Bronze Age Denmark where the first Bronze Age textile discovery occurred in 1871 in the parish of Borum, west of Aarhus in Jutland. There was a large earthen barrow in this district which was 6m high and

38m in diameter. The local people decided that this was a waste of good earth and that it would do their crops the world of good if they spread it over their fields. So they proceeded to cart away the earth to this purpose during the course of 1871. After much earth extraction, a large oak tree was discovered in the mound. This was of no interest to the Danish farmers so they simply drove their carts over the oak tree until it started to become a nuisance to them, whereupon they set about moving it out of the way. As they started to move what they thought was just a fallen tree, it split open to reveal the skeleton of a woman. In fact, it was an oak coffin containing what was later found to be a Bronze Age woman. The bones were well preserved and the clothing and grave goods were a revelation to the simple farmers who discovered them. Two more coffins were later found in this barrow, one for an old man, and the other for a younger man. It is because of the unique wet conditions that this and many other Danish Bronze Age bodies are so well preserved. The coffins had been placed on a pile of stones and usually thousands of years of rainfall ooze through the barrow, and the organic materials decompose and the metals oxidize. However, in this and many other cases in Denmark, water had been trapped at the bottom of the barrow because of the high water table, thus preventing oxygen from degrading the artefacts. In addition, the coffins were made of oak, a long-lasting wood which has the effect of preserving the contents of objects made from it.

The woman was thought to be about 60 years old, her hair was blonde and plaited, she wore a tailored woollen jacket and a simple skirt. There was the stain of what had been a bronze disk above her waist, attached to a very elaborate belt. At the time, this belt was described as being a masterpiece of textile-making with two elaborate tassels on the end. One of the most interesting finds in the coffin was the unusual hairnet made by a twisted-wool technique which is known in Denmark as 'sprang' (**12**). A similar technique has been found in coptic graves in Egypt, and is still in use today by primitive cultures in parts of South America — the technique is very similar to the game of 'cats cradle'. Threads on a frame are twisted together with the fingers to create either a simple or intricate loose net.

In 1921 another barrow was being dismantled by farmers at Ectvd in Jutland and another hollowed-out oak tree trunk coffin was found, this one being 2m in length. The coffin lid in this barrow was so tight-fitting that not a particle of earth had squeezed its way inside and everything was found exactly as it had been when laid to rest in the Bronze Age. Inside was a fur cover of cowhide which had been spread out over the bottom of the coffin with the fur side up and folded over the body before the coffin lid was sealed. When this cover was pulled back, the body of a young girl was found, her loose blonde hair covering her face. She was dressed in a short jacket with elbow length sleeves. At her waist, a circular bronze disk and horn comb were fastened to her belt which had a large tassel on it and at her feet was a birch bark container (see **colour plate 9**). Below the belt was a skirt of cords,

The first metals: the Bronze Age

13 A typical bronze sword with some more of the author's roundhouses in the background

that reached to her knees and was wound round her body twice. This is a fascinating article of clothing, it looks like a string skirt and makes you think of Hawaiian dancing girls. She wore two bronze arm rings and a slender ring of bronze wire at her left ear.

There is widespread evidence of the day-to-day chores of Bronze Age farming settlements. The items found include saddle querns, which were stones used for grinding corn (**colour plate 12**). The saddle quern consists of a lower stone, the 'saddle stone', on which the corn was placed, and an upper stone, the 'rider stone', which was pushed to-and-fro on top of this and ground the corn. Also, loom weights are often found in excavated houses, indicating that these people used a warp-weighted loom for weaving their own cloth to wear or for trading.

Due to the general prosperity of the time, there became a pressing need to defend what one had, from others who wanted to take it. So an élite warrior class was formed to defend the metal workers, craftsmen, food producers and tradesmen. Bronze weapon-making became more elaborate between 1800 and 800 BC. Whereas daggers were made to begin with and the sword superseded them, there seemed to be a preference in some areas for the use of bronze spearheads. In Europe, bronze helmets and shields were produced but it is not known if these were actually worn in battle or just made to impress for ceremonial purposes.

Recent research is now challenging the idealistic viewpoint, that swords were merely for ceremonial purposes and not for actual warfare (**13**). In an article in *British Archaeology*, Sue Bridgford suggests that these swords were actually used in group combat. Having examined several hundred swords, she says that the majority bear the signs of blade-on-blade combat and tend to have numerous nicks and wave-like distortions on the edges.

The evidence for the emergence of mighty chieftains is seen in the new practice of individuals being buried in tumuli, or burial mounds. Richly-equipped men and women were buried in these mounds, with bronze or gold objects and luxury items. Men of wealth and power were often buried with weapons and, in many cases, a razor, a needle and tweezers made out of bone. Women were adorned with armlets and bracelets of gold and other jewellery. Bush Barrow, discovered in 1808 and 1km from the newly refurbished Bronze Age Stonehenge, is a good example of such barrows. Inside was the skeleton of a man who had three daggers, one of which had a handle decorated with hundreds of gold nails or studs. He also had a decorated mace-head that could have been a sign of his office in the community. Generally though, throughout Europe, there was a new type of burial for the common people too. People were cremated and their bones and ashes were placed in a particular type of large pot called a 'collared urn' (**14**). These urns were then placed in a stone cist and turned upside down before being covered with a stone and buried in cemeteries called urn-fields. Monoliths also became more common in Europe and stone circles and stone rows were erected.

14 Reconstructions made by the author of Bronze Age funerary urns

These rows tended to be aligned to the north-east and the south-west to catch the rising and the setting of the sun. The building of Stonehenge and other such monuments seem to show a preoccupation with the movement of the sun and possibly the stars.

One of the most fascinating features of Stonehenge is the fact that the stones known as 'bluestone' that built it came from south Wales, some 240 miles away. There have been many theories as to how these vast stones were transported, but I feel the best is a new concept that the stones were floated right up to the site on barges. In a paper by Andrew Sherratt, it is suggested that the Upper and Lower River Avon, which cuts across the land from the Bristol Channel to Devizes, might in the past have been linked to the River Avon to the south of Stonehenge, which then travels down to Hengistbury Head and the south coast. The Upper Avon links to the Lower Avon at the top of the Severn Estuary, and within a few miles of Stonehenge is the East Avon. If, in the Bronze Age, these rivers were in fact linked, not only would it be relatively easy to transport the stones from south Wales to the site at Stonehenge, but it would also link Ireland and Wales, both rich in gold, to the known emporium at Hengistbury Head — a place where it is thought goods were stored prior to transport over the Channel to Europe. Maybe the wealthy Wessex culture, with no apparent produce to sell or minerals to trade, became rich due to this river traffic. Perhaps the Wessex chiefs exacted a toll on the gold miners of Wales and Ireland with a Bronze Age type Suez Canal. The linking of the three rivers would easily have been possible to the builders of Stonehenge. As well as having some unknown ritual purpose, Stonehenge could have been a status symbol to show any passing traders just how powerful these Wessex chieftains were. We will probably never know but it is an interesting hypothesis.

Around 1200 BC some catastrophic event happened to the climate the Bronze Age farmers enjoyed. It appears from the archaeological record that all upland settlements were suddenly abandoned; why this should be so is much debated in the archaeological world, although it does appear that sudden climatic change must have had something to do with it. In 1159 BC it is known that a volcano called Hekla, off the coast of Iceland, erupted with extraordinary force. This is accepted because a thin layer of volcanic ash has been found for this period over northern Europe. It is possible that the large amount of sulphur sent into the atmosphere would have come down as acid rain, making acid soil areas impossible to farm. Crops would fail and the dust in the atmosphere could have blocked out the sun and created low pressure, which would in turn increase the amount of rainfall. By 1000 BC there were definite indications that the mild, warm climate of the Neolithic and Bronze Ages was changing. It became cooler and wetter, and large tracts of blanket bog appeared in the upland regions, making it impossible to farm land that had been in the past. What cannot be ignored is that this new climatic change happened about 150 years after the Icelandic volcano erupted. The migration of the large upland populations to the already cultivated areas in the lowlands was inevitable. This migration south must have brought an overwhelming pressure on the lowlanders to protect their lands from these refugees. It is also about this time that once open settlements become defended with palisades and ditches, and the first hill forts appear. It has been suggested, however, that the hill forts were not just to protect the people in the outlying settlements in time of war, but were market centres for trading goods from one community to another. Each community developed and prospered during this later Bronze Age period in spite of migration and there was little real change to the status quo until the emergence of a new and even more useful metal in around 800 BC — iron.

5 The Iron Age

The use of iron was an important step forward in European development, not just because it was a harder metal, but because the ore was so widely available and did not even have to be mined since it was found on the surface of the earth. Although iron required higher temperatures to smelt, it did not need to be mixed with another metal as did bronze. The first peoples known to have used iron were the Hittites in western Asia between 2000 and 1400 BC, and the first true Iron Age society in Europe was the Hallstatt culture from the Austrian Alps. These people were primarily salt miners and traders who worked mines near Salzburg, on the western shore of Lake Hallstatt. Salt was important to the Neolithic and Bronze Age societies as a trading commodity. The hunter-gatherers had no need of salt, as there were salts in the meat they ate which was usually roasted and not boiled. Once meat was boiled and grains were eaten, salt was needed to make it palatable. As the people farmed the land farther inland, the distances to the salt-producing centres on the coast were greater so inland salt mines, as at Hallstatt, became increasingly important and traders would have travelled great distances to supply the demand. It is possibly because of this trade that they were the first to import the new iron-working technology to Europe from the east. In 1876, the Vienna Academy of Sciences excavated some of the salt-working sites and in his study of the role of salt in the economy of prehistory, Jacques Nenquin commented:

> . . . a number of objects have been discovered in the mine galleries of Hallstatt which have proved to be of great importance for the study of prehistoric man. Fragments of clothing made of leather, wool or linen are known and leather caps, shoes and even a sort of leather gloves, probably used as protection for their hands when the miners slid down ropes leading to the galleries. Mention must be made of the remains of food, like barley, millet, beans, and a cultivated form of apple and cherry, fragments of pottery wooden dishes and spoons of wood and so on. On the surface traces of wooden huts were found repeatedly. These tunnels burrowed to a depth of 1000 feet (305m) into the mountainside. Leather bags made of cowhide stretched over a wooden frame were used to carry the salt to the surface.

15 Drawing of a bronze couch found at Hochdorf, Germany

A huge cemetery was found at Hallstatt, consisting of more than 2500 graves. Due to the salty environment the grave goods were found in remarkably well-preserved condition and it is thanks to the interest in these grave finds by the then director of the mine in the late 1800s that this site is so well known today. It is because of this vast graveyard, with iron goods and exotic trade goods, that the first Iron Age period is called the Hallstatt period. The wealth of this salt-mining culture is evident in some of the finery with which the people were buried. Imported materials showed trading links with Etruria, Greece and with Rome. Italian metal objects are found with amber from the Baltic and even Egyptian influences can be found. In these graves, the style of burial could be thought to be Etruscan in manner. The body, burnt or unburnt, was laid under a four-wheeled wagon in a wooden chamber under a grave mound. There was a preponderance of horse trappings in these graves, indicating a close relationship with horses, yet they did not appear to be buried with them as found in the archaeology of the steppes of Russia. This rich Hallstatt culture spread during the next few hundred years over most of northern Europe and the period known as that of the Hallstatt Princes began. This conclusion is formed by the emergence of aristocratic graves near to the common graves that were obviously for the working classes. The most fantastic aristocratic grave in my opinion is the wagon burial at Hochdorf in Germany. A ritual cart and a complete dinner service in gold and bronze was deposited in this wealthy man's grave. He was richly dressed and wore a birch-bark cap and lay on a bronze couch (**15**). This couch is truly magnificent, it could seat three people and was made of sheet bronze, richly decorated and resting on four pairs of legs. The legs at the front were cast figures of men and between their legs were wheels, very much like a man riding a unicycle — this couch was dated to about 600 BC. These aristocrats, known as the Hallstatt Princes, spread their culture to all corners of northern Europe from Britain to Denmark through Germany, Hungary, southern Bohemia, and on to Yugoslavia, Spain and France.

The La Tène and Belgic Celts

In about 500 BC the Hallstatt culture seems to have come to an end in mainland Europe; the typical Hallstatt features in the archaeological landscape just stop. Nobody seems to know why, but at this time the first Hallstatt period began in Britain. This is, however, about the time that Rome became a republic and maybe it was a good time to move out of this emerging Empire's reach, although it seems highly unlikely that such a dominant society would just move out of Europe. We can only base our knowledge of prehistoric times on the archaeology and, until someone finds something that tells a different story, we have to assume the Hallstatt culture came to some demise around this period in Europe. At the time of the demise of the Hallstatt appears a new culture, the La Tène. These people came from the lake villages of Switzerland and are best known for their decorative metalwork and its distinctive style of elaborate spiral and circular patterns — this is the style that is generally recognised as 'Celtic'. The next 300 years saw the expansion of these Celtic peoples through Europe and Ireland, the culture reaching Britain about a hundred years after the Hallstatt influence. The lake village of Glastonbury in Somerset is a typical La Tène-influenced community. The house structures are similar to the ones in Switzerland and the artefacts found, particularly the pottery, has the stylised La Tène patterning on it. Due to the site being in the middle of a peat area, it is one of the best-preserved Iron Age settlements in Britain. This phase of the Iron Age Celts lasted in Britain until about 120 BC when a new band of Celts arrived from Belgium, the Belgic Celts. Probably due to Roman pressure on their own lands, many immigrated to the still Roman-free Britain. They landed in Kent and Essex and aggressively took the lands of the Celts who were living there. In the classical world, the Belgic Celts had a reputation for being particularly warlike even by normal Celtic standards. Strabo says about them

> Of these people they say that the Belgae are the bravest... consequently they alone could hold out against the onset of the Germans. As for the largeness of the population, this is an indication: it is found upon enquiry they say, that there are as many as three hundred thousand of those Belgae who are able to bear arms.

Although these three types of Celts, Hallstatt, La Tène and Belgae, had different styles in their metalwork, art and dwellings, such as the lake dwellings of

16 Stage one of making a furnace in which to smelt iron

17 Stage two: the smelting of the iron ore which is kept burning for 16 hours. The furnace is then broken apart to reveal the iron ore

the La Tène, they were all Celts. They all had the same personality traits as the classical writers tell us and the same druidical religion and laws.

Iron smelting and production

Iron was obtained by collecting the ore, washing it and then placing it in a clay furnace. A charcoal fire was lit in the furnace and a simple blast tunnel made out of fire-clay was used. A pair of skin bellows was attached to the funnel and the fire was bellowed for many hours until a temperature high enough to melt the ore out of the rock was obtained. The next day, the clay furnace would have been broken apart to reveal the lumps of metal amidst large quantities of slag or waste (**16 & 17**). These pieces of metal were fused again in another fire and hammered to the required shape. This heating and hammering is just the same as the old blacksmith used to do in his forge until not too long ago. The Celts were said to have developed techniques combining hard and soft metals in a single implement, thereby making it more flexible yet with a hard cutting edge. In parts of Scandinavia they collected the ore from the peat bogs; this ore was a refined type of iron and easier to smelt as there was not so much slag or waste with it when it was smelted. Diodorus Siculus describes the particular skills of the Celtiberians in making swords.

> To make their weapons they bury plates of iron in the ground and leave them there until in the course of time the rust has eaten out what is weak in the iron and what is left is only the most unyielding, out of this they make their swords. These swords will cut through any helmet due to the exceptional quality of the iron.

The best ideas are the simplest and this is a prime example of this. The simplicity of burying the plates of iron so that the impurities will rust out is, a stroke of genius — obvious in hindsight but not so easy to think of in the first place. Iron was fashioned into many day-to-day objects, such as fire dogs which were frames used in pairs to keep logs off the ground making them burn better. They were also used to suspend meat over the fire to spit roast it. Iron was used to tip spades and the simple ploughs of the period. This meant that deeper furrows could be ploughed and previously un-tillable land with heavy clay soils could be brought into production. Axes and simple saws were made of this new metal which also helped agricultural development because larger areas of forest could be cut down and brought into production too. Houses could be made using iron nails instead of drilling large holes and inserting pegs made of wood into them. So, as a result, food production increased and with it, the Celtic population.

Transportation and roads

According to the archaeological data, trading between the Hallstatt Celts was widespread and much use was made of rivers as transportation arteries to many areas. Yet it is well known that these people were skilled chariot riders and horsemen. There is also the evidence from the Hallstatt graveyard, that four-wheeled wagons were an important part of their culture. Strabo mentions the Hallstatt salt miners producing salt meat or bacon to export to all parts of Italy. So the preponderance of wagons must indicate that there were roads on which to drive them. Ancient Bronze Age trade routes to supply Europe with tin from Cornwall became utilized in the Iron Age to transport wine, olive oil and fish products to Britain. Archaeology shows from the remains of amphorae that the luxury foodstuffs of Roman occupied Gaul were becoming popular with the independent Celts of Britain.

We were all taught at school that the Romans were the first to make roads in Europe which were good enough to transport wagons and heavy loads. This is a great misconception. Four-wheeled wagons need reasonably good roads to travel on otherwise they will soon become impassable. There has also been the suggestion by some academics that if the pre-Roman Celts *did* transport their wares about Europe in wagons, then they must have confined their routes to areas of flat dry plains. Not so, as the archaeological evidence in Ireland shows. At Corlea in County Longford, a great wooden roadway was discovered traversing a marshland. It was a massive construction, extending for 2km and made of huge oak planks, 3.5-4m in length. These were laid down edge-to-edge on supporting pairs of longitudinal runners. This trackway, dated to 148 BC, was intended for the use of large wheeled vehicles. The labour and skill required for such a huge undertaking — to say nothing of the hundreds of massive oak trees needed in its construction — shows quite clearly that road-making in any terrain was well within the capabilities of the Celts. Although the Romans may have constructed some new roadways in Europe to take their troops to specific areas, they mainly put their stone paving on top of the original Celtic wagon ways and posterity has credited them as being the first road-builders of Europe. Instead, it would be more appropriate I feel, to call them road improvers.

War and hill forts

Warfare was a way of life to the Celts. It was a way of testing the courage and skill of their young men — and perhaps their young women — for it is said that the Celtic society had full equality of the sexes, and if a woman wanted to fight she could. This was displayed when Queen Boudicca of the Iceni tribe in Britain was said to have led an army of 230,000 Celts as she attempted to drive the Romans out of Britain. So honoured was the warrior in Celtic society that a strict etiquette was maintained when dining after a battle. Athenaeus mentions the tradition of the Hero's portion.

> And in former times, when the hindquarters were served up, the bravest hero took the thigh piece, and if another man claimed it they stood up and fought in single combat to the death.

The Celts were said to love a good fight and would start one at the least provocation. The Classical historian Athenaeus says of the Celts:

> The Celts sometimes engage in single combat at dinner. Assembling in arms they engage in a mock battle-drill and mutual thrust and parry. But sometimes wounds are inflicted, and the irritation caused by this may lead even to the slaying of the opponent, unless the bystanders hold

them back. The whole race, which is now called Celtic, is madly fond of war, high-spirited and quick to battle, but otherwise straightforward and not of evil character. And so when they are stirred up they assemble in their bands for battle, quite openly and without forethought. For at any time or place, and on whatever pretext you stir them up, you will have them ready to face danger, even if they have nothing on their side but their own strength and courage.

When fighting in battle the sword was the favoured weapon, accompanied by a broad iron spear. Although it is known that bows and arrows and slingshots were used by the Celts, it was the sword and spear that reigned supreme in their armoury. The shield was also an important part of the Celts equipment for war. Siculus again says of the Celtiberians:

> ... the Lusitanians who carry in war very small shields which are interwoven with cords of sinew and are able to protect the body very well.

Some accounts talk about shields made of wood or of wicker, like a flat basket disk. Siculus, when describing the Gauls and the Germans says:

> For their armour they use long shields, as high as a man with figures of animals embossed on them in bronze. On their heads they put bronze helmets, in some cases horns are attached to them.

The famous Battersea shield is a fine example of a Celtic shield made of sheet bronze and inlayed with coloured enamel. It shows that the Celts were just as much preoccupied with the look of an object as with its usefulness. The two main fighting methods used by the Celts were on chariots and single combat with swords. The light, two-wheeled chariots were pulled by specially bred ponies and were much admired by the Romans. The fittings were made of bronze, the top part of the frame was sometimes made of wicker to make it lighter and the wheels were made of wood with a rim of iron. When Siculus first describes the inhabitants of Britain he says:

> They use chariots for instance in their wars, even as tradition tells us the ancient Greeks did in the Trojan wars.

When invading Britain, Caesar describes this practice in the writings of the historian Dio Cassius.

18 Artistic impression of the invasion of Mona

> The Romans upon meeting them were at first thrown into confusion by the attack of their chariots.

It also seems to have been the practice to throw their adversaries into confusion in many ways before a fight. Basically, they liked to undermine their opponent's confidence first to get an advantage in battle. Siculus comments on this practice:

> And when someone accepts their challenge to battle they proudly recite the deeds of valour of their ancestors and proclaim their own valorous quality at the same time abusing and making little of their opponent and generally attempting to rob him beforehand of his fighting spirit.

The most impressive example of this practice is the quotation from Tacitus about the attack on the Isle of Mona (Anglesey) during the beginning of the Roman occupation of Britain. From his headquarters in Roman Chester, Suetonius Paulinus commanded the invasion of Mona:

He prepared accordingly to attack the island of Mona which has a considerable population of its own, while serving as a haven for refugees; and in view of the shallow and variable channel, constructed a flotilla of boats with flat bottoms. By this method the infantry crossed; the cavalry, who followed, did so by fording or, in deeper water, by swimming at the side of their horses. On the beach stood the adverse array, a serried mass of arms and men, with women flitting between the ranks. In the style of Furies, in robes of deathly black with dishevelled hair, they brandished torches; while a circle of druids, lifting their hands to heaven and showering imprecations. This site struck the troops with such awe at the extraordinary spectacle that as though their limbs were paralysed, they exposed their bodies to wounds without an attempt at movement. Then, reassured by their general, and inciting to them never to flinch before a band of females and fanatics, they charged behind the standards, cut down all who met them, and enveloped the enemy in his own flames. The next step was to install a garrison among the conquered population, and to demolish the groves consecrated to their savage cults. (**18**)

This description sums up the Celts' valiant attitude to warfare. Even when the odds were ten-to-one against them, proud and fearless they went into battle. This quotation conjures up a picture of a very important moment in the history of the Celts: this attack on Mona was not just an attack on a group of Celtic refugees. It was an assault on the main seat of learning of the druid priests of Europe. All the time Caesar was trying to keep the Gaelic Celts subjugated, the druids would fire them up from their sanctuary on Mona. As the troops stood paralysed on the shore and were cut down, the future of druids in Europe was held in the balance. When the spell was broken, under the encouragement of their general, the druids of Anglesey and their ancient oak groves were destroyed forever.

Since this preoccupation with tribal warfare was part of the character of the Celts, they needed to live in defended settlements, or at least to have some sort of available fortress in the area in which the tribe's people could seek refuge in times of conflict. Hill forts are therefore a common feature in Iron Age archaeology. In fact, there is much more evidence in the archaeology of hill forts than in private dwellings. This is mainly because so much effort was put into the construction of these defended areas. The basic principal of the defensive fort was a stockade, a bank and ditch, or a wall. They could be just large enough to defend a small tribal family or a whole town and all their stock; in some cases the defended areas were hundreds of acres in size. There is an account by Dio Cassius about Caesar's second expedition to Britain that suggests that the Celts in warfare used a mixture of guerrilla tactics and temporary stockades near their battlegrounds, only retreating to the permanent fortress when defeated by overwhelming odds. This is the passage in question:

> ... they proceeded to annoy the Romans' foraging parties. Indeed after being defeated in a certain battle on open ground they drew the invaders in pursuit to their retreat and killed many in their turn ... but being defeated by the cavalry, withdrew to the Thames where they encamped after cutting off the ford by means of stakes, some under water. But Caesar by a powerful assault forced them to leave the stockade, and later on by siege drove them from their fortresses.

On the whole, Celtic fortresses seem to have been built to take advantage of natural features, such as steep escarpments, cliff lines, rock faces or coastal promontories. They were generally built on high ground so that the defenders would immediately be aware of approaching enemies. In peacetime these forts could have been used as markets and trading centres but were always there if a community and their livestock needed protection from attacking neighbours. One of the largest hill forts, which is still intact, is at Maiden Castle in Dorset. It has multiple ditches and was thought to originally have been a causeway camp in the Neolithic period, but it was renovated and expanded in 300 BC and has an area of 18 hectares (or 45 acres). There are four lines of ditches and ramparts going up the hill, two entrances and, on the summit, there is evidence of a cluster of dwellings. At another fort at Uffington in Berkshire, a stylised horse was cut out of the turf on the limestone hillside. It is 109m long by 40m high and no doubt represented the insignia of the tribe that lived in the fort above it. One can imagine this horse painted on the shields of the tribe that lived in this fortress. Maybe many slopes on the approaches to hill forts were labelled in this way.

Celtic society and culture

From the accounts of the classical writers the Celts seemed to be a strikingly handsome race. Their appearance is described by the Roman writer, Ammianus Marcelinus

> Almost all the Celts are tall in stature, their hair is not naturally blond, but they use artificial means to increase the natural quality of colour. For they continually wash their hair in lime wash and draw it back from their forehead to the crown and the nape of the neck. The hair is so thickened by this that it differs in no way to a horse mane.

Girls seemed to be admired if they had very long hair, which was plaited and was wound round their heads, or sometimes left loose. The men shaved their faces but let their moustaches grow. Warriors sometimes tattooed their body and, to make themselves look more fierce in battle, were said to paint their whole body with blue woad dye. Cleanliness was a very important part of the Celtic way of life. Unlike the people of the Mediterranean world, who were content to anoint themselves with oil and then scrape it off, the Celts invented soap to wash themselves. There were also health laws in Celtic society, although they may be a result of their collective vanity as a people; Strabo observes,

> . . . they endeavour not to grow fat or pot-bellied and any young man who exceeds the standard measure of the girdle is punished.

So becoming too fat was against the Celtic law and punishable by fines. Not the sort of law one would imagine uncouth barbarians (as the Romans described them) as having.

It is quite well known today that the Celts were said to have a fondness for tartans and plaid fabrics in their clothes (**colour plate 11**). This is true but they also had a love for the flamboyant when it came to dress. Strabo observed:

> The clothing they wear is striking, shirts which have been dyed and embroidered in varied colours. Heavy material in the winter, light in the summer, these are set checks close together in varied colours. Some of them gather their shirts with belts plaited with gold and silver.

Trousers, as worn by the Celtic men, were an entirely novel concept to the toga-clad Romans. In fact, they adopted the use of trousers for their own cavalry, as many of the best cavalrymen in the Roman Empire had been recruited from the Celts. The Romans seemed amazed at the ostentation of their appearance, making it very easy for them to identify a group of Celts in a crowded town anywhere in the Empire. Here is one of my favourite quotations about the Celts' clothing; it is amazing how infrequently it is quoted in books about them; Strabo again:

> . . . In addition to their trait of simplicity and high spiritedness, that of witlessness and boastfulness is much in evidence, and also that of fondness for ornaments; for they not only wear golden ornaments both chains round their necks and bracelets round arms and wrists, but their dignitaries wear garments that are dyed in colours and sprinkled with gold.

Sprinkling gold onto a woollen garment is not as impractical as you might think. Gold dust sticks to wool like glue and once sprinkled on the coloured cloak would not come off unless it was washed when, of course, great care would have been taken to sieve the washing water. The legends of the Golden Fleece of Greek mythology has its roots in fact; it was the Greek practice to lay woollen fleeces in the gold-bearing streams with the wool side down. When lifted out of the stream after the required time, the fleece would shimmer with encrusted gold dust. The fleeces were then burnt in a hearth and all that was left was the gold. Maybe the Celtic traders watched this practice in Greece and thought it not just a good way to acquire gold dust but a wonderful way to wear their beloved gold.

Religion and laws played an important part in Celtic society. These laws were for all aspects of their daily lives. Strabo looks at Celtic society when he says:

> As for their custom relating to the men and the women (I mean the fact that their tasks have been exchanged in a manner opposite to what obtains among us) it is one which they share in common with many other barbarian peoples. Among all the Gaelic peoples, generally speaking, there are three sets of men who are held in exceptional honour; the Bards, the Vates, and the druids. The Bards are singers and poets; the Vates diviners and natural philosophers; while the druids, in addition to natural philosophy study also moral philosophy. The druids are considered the most just of men, and on this account they are entrusted with the decision, not only of the private disputes, but the public disputes as well; so that, in former times they even arbitrated cases of war and made the opponents stop when they were about to line up for battle, and the murder cases in particular, had been turned over to them for decision... However, not only the druids, but others as well say that men's souls and also the universe are indestructible, although both fire and water will at some time or other prevail over them.

The Celts had no tradition of writing so they cultivated an oral memory tradition; all the laws and traditions had to be handed down orally from one generation to the next. A Druid-elect was thought to take 20 years to master and fully assimilate the secrets of his calling. These Druidical priests, however, carried out their ritual practices only in natural places such as groves of oak trees that they thought particularly sacred. Pliny describes a ceremony of the druids:

> ... groves of hard oaks are chosen even for their own sake, and the magicians (druids) perform no rites without using foliage of the trees, so that it may be supposed that it is from this custom that they get the name druid from the Greek word meaning 'oak', but further anything growing on oak trees they think to have been sent down from heaven and to be a sign that the particular tree has been chosen by God

himself. Mistletoe is however rather seldom found on hard oak and when it is discovered it is gathered with great ceremony, and particularly on the sixth day of the moon. Hailing the moon in a native word meaning 'healing all things', they prepare a ritual sacrifice and banquet beneath a tree . . . A priest arrayed in white vestments climbs the tree and with a golden sickle cuts down the mistletoe which is caught in a white cloak.

Of the druids of Britain he says:

> At the present day Britannia is still fascinated by magic, and performs its rites with so much ceremony that it almost seems as though it was she who had imparted the cult to the Persians.

Obviously, Pliny was amazed at the meticulous detail of their rites, thinking it strange that barbarians should be so particular. There is some evidence for either ritual sacrifice or execution in the remains of the bodies that have been found in peat bogs from around Europe. From Lindow man in Cheshire to Tollund man, Grauballe man in Denmark and many more, most these bodies are pegged down in the marshes. They have been either strangled or had their throats cut. Due to the wonderful preserving qualities of the peat, these bodies were discovered intact — so much so that even their stomach contents could be analysed. In all cases, it appeared that the men ate a last meal of some sort of grain gruel full of weed or wild herb seeds and large quantities of chaff. It has been suggested by some that this was the typical food of the Celtic period but as we will see later, this is far from being the case — the bones from the middens testify to this. Some also think that there is some type of ritual significance in the types of weed seeds found in the gruel. However, there is another school of thought which may be more plausible and that is that the chaff-rich, weed-seedy grain gruel was, in fact, floor sweepings, just prison food for criminals condemned to death for some sordid crime. Tacitus throws light on this practice in his studies of the Germans:

> The traitor and deserter are hanged on trees, the coward, the shirker and the unnaturally vicious are drowned in miry swamps under cover of wattled hurdles. The distinction in the punishment implies that deeds of violence should be paid for in the full glare of publicity, but that deeds of shame should be suppressed.

If the bodies were pegged down, which they undoubtedly were, then they certainly were not fitting sacrifices to the gods.

Druidical festivals were an important part of the Celts' lives and therefore very well planned and executed. The Celtic year was divided into four parts around four major festivals: the first (and the Celtic New Year) was the festival of Samain on the first of November each year. The present-day tradition of Halloween is on the exact same night as the Celtic New Year's Eve, a time to reflect on the past and the spirits of friends and relatives gone. The next festival was that of Imbolc on the first of February, still celebrated in Ireland as St Brigett's day and thought to be, in some way, a part of the first ewe's milk coming and a renewal of spring festival. The third event was Beltane, meaning beautiful fire festival, on the first of May. We still celebrate May Day as a spring festival but to the Celts it had an important significance as a cleansing festival before the new season. The fires in their houses were said to have been kept going all year round, up to the eve of Beltane. This was the day when the old fire was put out and a new fire made with a fire-bow or flint and iron to last the whole year. Two fires were said to be made in the village and all the animals walked through them in a cleansing ceremony. Maybe all the grass baskets and bedding was also put onto these fires so as to cleanse not just spiritually but also physically. I think this festival in particular has its roots in some Celtic health plan to rid their dwellings and animals of pests that had been acquired during the winter months. There are many herbs that grow in the marshlands, such as fleabane, which are pesticides when burnt; these could well have been added to the Beltane fires. The fourth, the biggest and the last festival was Lugnasa, on the first of August. This was the central day of this festival because it was said to start 15 days before the first of August and last 15 days after. The Roman writers were amazed at the preparations for this festival and commented on the large barns packed with wine and food for this grand party. It is well recorded that the Celts were very fond of wine and beer, so much so that Strabo writes of how much they would be prepared to give for a flagon:

> These people have such a love for wine that great profits are made by merchants. They are said to even exchange a slave for a jar of wine.

Athenaeus however observes:

> ... the wheat beer prepared with honey in Gaul is drunk by the poorer classes.

So to summarise the Celts: they were a flamboyant people who loved wine and a good fight. They treated their women as equals and believed their souls lasted forever. No wonder there is such a revival in all things Celtic, they seemed to be a people who lived life to the full, enjoying themselves as much as the whim might take them.

6 Bread

Bread, the staple of life, is mentioned many times by classical writers and it may be assumed that since the discovery of bread in early Neolithic finds in Europe, it was the staple of prehistoric diets too (**19**). A rare example is a loaf of yeasted bread made of finely-ground barley and wheat flours discovered in the late Neolithic levels at Lake Bienne in Switzerland. Until this discovery, it was widely assumed that prehistoric people did not have yeasted bread. The impression that prehistoric peoples ate hard, barely-chewable pieces of unleavened bread is just the type of misconception that will be dispelled in this book. In ancient Egypt, half-baked bread was soaked in water and date juice before being added to flour to make fresh bread. This principle is still used in many parts of northern Europe today to make sourdough bread — a little dough is taken from each batch of bread to be added to the next to keep particular yeasts alive.

Yeast production has always been linked with the brewing of beer and wine — the interdependence between grain, yeast, bread and fermenting liquor has persisted throughout history. Further testimony for the link between brewing and baking was found on the Egyptian Ben-Hasan site in a tomb of the Middle Kingdom, dated to 2000 BC, where archaeologists discovered a wooden model of a brewery and bakehouse attached together.

Certain fruits such as the grape and the elderberry are host to large amounts of wild yeast on their skins. Fermenting wine or beer can be added to flour to produce leavened bread. Pliny commented about this practice

> When the corn of Gaul and Spain of the kinds we have stated is steeped to make beer the foam that forms on the surface in the process is for leaven, in consequence of which those races have a lighter kind of bread than others.

This is not the opinion we generally have of the bread baked by 'barbarian' Celts. One would normally assume that the Roman bread was lighter and finer than that of the Celts but, if this were so, Pliny would presumably have made a point of stating this. It is well known that the Celts in particular were very fond of wine and beer. Strabo the classical writer comments that

19 Bread dough ready to be cooked on a granite stone on the fire

> They also drink beer; but are scarce of wine and what wine they have made they speedily drink up in merry feastings with their kinsfolk.

The fermenting of grain to make alcohol is thought to have begun at the same time as the first cultivation of grain. The growing of grain had become widespread between Iran and Turkey 10,000 years ago. In ancient Mesopotamian texts from the third millennium BC, there are said to be a list of 19 different types of beer made according to the combinations of grains and herbs used in their manufacture. Yet cultivated grain does not seem to appear in northern Europe until the Neolithic, approximately 6,000 years ago. In Britain a small number of grain impressions have been found on Neolithic pottery at the Abingdon causeway enclosure in Oxfordshire, which give us concrete evidence that emmer wheat and six-row barley were cultivated in some quantity during this period. However, widespread evidence of grain cultivation in Britain is not found until the Bronze Age, approximately 3,500 years ago. I am often asked how prehistoric people might have discovered the process of beer-making. I believe it has a lot to do with the storage of grain in pits. The classical historian Diodorus Siculus comments on how the Ancient Britons harvested their grain

> They dwell in mean cottages, covered for the most part with reeds or sticks. In the reaping of their corn, they cut off the ears from the stalks, and so house them in repositories underground.

There is widespread archaeological evidence for these grain storage pits throughout Europe. These pits vary in shape and size over different regions but the basic principle is the same. A large hole is dug into the ground, most commonly a bell shape, essentially a large rounded hole with a narrow neck at the top. Grain is poured into the pit after the harvest and presumably a plug of clay was used to cover it, followed by a layer of turf on top to stop the clay from drying out. Although there is no evidence for these clay plugs, they are the most logical top for the pits and could have been ploughed out over the centuries to leave no traces of their existence. The grain on the edges of the pit was in contact with the damp earth and so began to germinate. As it did so, the germination process used up all the remaining oxygen in the sealed pit and released carbon dioxide in exchange. When the oxygen was exhausted, the germinating grain died and formed a crust on the outer edge of the pit. The grain within was sealed in a vacuum and would keep for years without deteriorating. Some research into the use of this type of storage pit was undertaken by Dr. Reynolds at Butser Ancient Farm in the 1970s. It was found that grain stored for a year in a pit was actually in better condition than grain stored in a modern, electrically-heated granary for the same period of time.

One side-effect of the pit storage is that in the following spring, when most of the grain had been removed and used, what remained would begin to germinate. Germinating wheat and barley taste very pleasant, much like liquorice, and I am sure this would have been a popular food during the springtime. Unfortunately, it is only at the early stages of germination that it tastes good. If left a week too long the germinating grain goes mouldy and is wasted as a food. It is not unrealistic to assume that someone made an attempt to preserve this sprouting grain by drying it in a kiln. Once baked the grain sprouts change to malt — a completely different and very pleasant-smelling food. It also becomes a very important food as there are more vitamins and minerals in the malted grain than in its un-sprouted state. This is because sprouting grain releases the plant's energy supply of sugars and starches in order to make a new plant. This malted grain, when ground to a flour on a quern and added to water makes an enjoyable malt drink. It is also not too hard to imagine that this refreshing, tasty drink would have been made in large quantities and a surplus might have been left for another day. This would have started to ferment and the additional possibilities of alcohol discovered. There is now evidence from Iron Age Denmark of the malt-making process: in a burnt-down house at the Osterbolle settlement in Jutland, archaeologists discovered two clay pots containing sprouted barley. One was next to the hearth so it was ready to be dried and the other was set away from the heat to continue sprouting.

Connecting the growing of grains to the production of beer — and yeasted bread almost as a by-product — gives us a totally different perspective on the staple foods of prehistoric Europe; the assumption has always been that because the Romans built roads and cities, they must have had a finer diet than the barbarians they came to civilise.

The cultivation of these cereal crops however, was interdependent with the domestication of animals. Professor Andrew Sherratt wrote a ground-breaking paper in 1981 about how the domestication of animals meant much more to prehistoric societies than merely having handy sources of meat and milk:

> Although cattle were fully domesticated at least by the sixth millennium BC, they were not systematically used as traction animals until the later fourth millennium, when a specific technology was developed to make use of this. The most important applications were to the plough and the cart. The plough increased production and made economic the cultivation of a range of poor quality soils; it thus resulted in the colonisation of a wider area than had been possible under previous systems of cultivation. Both the ox-cart and the horse, as well as the pack-donkey, opened up the possibilities of bulk transport.

Large numbers of female animals would have been needed for milk, so there would have been a working stock and a breeding population of animals for these agricultural societies. Therefore the growing of cereal crops and the resulting need for large herds of draught animals would have occupied increasing amounts of the time of the first farmers. More substantial dwellings and storage facilities would be needed as a consequence.

The type of grain to be found carbonised in archaeological excavations in northern Europe are: barley (*Hordeum sp*), emmer wheat (*T. dicoccum*), einkorn wheat (*T. monococcum*), spelt wheat (*T. spelta*), oats (*Avens sp*), rye (*Secale cereale*) and millet (*Panicum milliaceum*).

As you can imagine, our modern bread wheat is very different from the prehistoric varieties, but not so much as far as the taste is concerned. The modern strains of wheat bear a much smaller grain than the ancient types and one would think that this would be the opposite, since we tend to develop crops to produce larger fruits in most other cases. There is a practical reason for developing a small, uniform grain and that is so that it can be harvested by machines. The small grain ripens quickly in the field and costs less to dry in granaries, it is also bred to ripen uniformly and easily shed its grain from the husk. Emmer wheat grains are twice as large as modern varieties and have to be processed by heating to displace the grain from its husk. This type of grain is most suited to hand harvesting so it was not so important for it to ripen evenly in the field. It will not become over-ripe and shed its grain, as will modern wheats if harvesting is delayed. If, by chance, emmer wheat is harvested a little under-ripe, it will slowly ripen in the husk whereas, if modern wheat is harvested under-ripe, it will overheat in the grain store and be spoiled.

The process of making grains into flours to bake bread was by using saddle querns in the Neolithic and Bronze Ages, and the more advanced rotary querns in the Iron Age. For the recipes using flour in this book, it is suggested that you use 100 per cent stone-ground wheat; however, in some large health food shops it is possible to find emmer, einkorn and spelt wheat flours. If you can get hold of these and want to be totally authentic, then use it wherever a recipe needs flour.

As previously mentioned, sprouted grains would have been a common commodity in an ancient settlement during the spring, so the first recipes use wheat sprouts.

Wheat sprouts

Take 125g of whole wheat grain, and soak it in water for 12 hours. Rinse and drain every day for about 10 days, keeping the container in a warm dark place. At the end of 10 days you will have a nutritious and tasty addition to a spring wild salad.

20 A Bronze Age quern on loan from the Royal Cornwall Museum

The sprouts taste very much like liquorice and children will eat them in large handfuls — so ensure that you make enough to begin with. Any grain can be sprouted in this way, the best-known of course being the barley sprouts that produce malt for bread and brewing. Wheat malt is just as good, although not commonly made today so here is a recipe for you to try.

Wheat malt

Spread some sprouts on a tray and bake in a moderate oven (the prehistoric equivalent would have been a clome oven). Keep turning the sprouts as they brown, when the sprouts are evenly brown and crisp take them out of the oven and cool. When cold, the wheat malt is ready to use. In prehistory it would have been ground between two flat stones (a quern) then stored until use. A food-processor will give you the same effect but is perhaps not quite as rewarding. The crisp, dry sprouts can be stored in an airtight container for many months until needed. In prehistory, a ceramic bowl sealed with a wooden stopper dipped into beeswax could have been used.

Malt bread (unleavened)

>   500g stone-ground flour
>   1 good cup of ground wheat malt
>   1 tsp sea salt
>   Water to mix

Mix the dry ingredients together and add enough water to make a soft dough. Shape into small round flat cakes and cook on a hot griddle until firm. (Makes 30)

Malt bread (leavened)

>   500g stone-ground flour
>   1 good cup of wheat malt
>   1 tsp sea salt
> $\frac{1}{2}$ cup fresh wild yeast or a piece of leaven★ (or 28g dried yeast)
>   Water to mix

Mix the dry ingredients together, then add the yeast and enough water to make a soft dough. Knead the dough until smooth and springy, then leave it in a warm place for three hours. Knead again, then shape into two loaves and leave on a tray to rise for another hour. Cook in a moderate oven until brown (about 45 minutes).

Both of these recipes can be made omitting the malt for a plain brown bread.
★ Wild yeast and leaven recipes can be found in Chapter 15, *Yeast, Wine, Beer and Teas*.

Oat and barley bread

> 750g medium oatmeal
> 750g barley flour
> 250 g butter
> 1 tsp sea salt
> Milk to mix

Mix the flours together then rub in the butter and add the salt. Mix to a soft dough with the milk. The oatmeal absorbs a lot of liquid, so do not make the dough too dry. Form into small cakes and cook on a hot griddle until firm and brown. This is a lovely savoury bread that is very good eaten with cheese.

Oatcakes (as still made in Scotland)

> 500g medium oatmeal
> 250g stone-ground wheat flour
> 56 g lard
> 1 tsp sea salt water to mix

Mix the flour and oatmeal together, add the salt and rub in the lard. Add enough water to make a dry dough and shape into flat cakes. Cook on a griddle until pale brown. When cold spread with butter or a slice of cheese.

Sweet bread

> 500g honey
> 1.5kg stone-ground flour
> 1 cup shelled chopped hazelnuts
> 1 tsp sea salt
> Milk to mix

Mix all the ingredients together with enough water to make a soft dough. Shape into small flat cakes and cook on a hot griddle that has been dusted with flour (this stops them from sticking). When cold, spread with butter.

Rich yeast spring bread

>   1kg stone-ground flour
>   500g butter
>   1 tsp salt
>   750g honey
>   1 cup wild yeast or leaven (or 28g dried yeast)
>   3 eggs (preferably duck)*
>   Milk to mix

Rub the butter into the flour and add the salt. Stir in the honey, eggs and yeast. Add enough milk to make a firm but soft dough and knead for five minutes. Leave in a warm place for three hours then knead again. Place on a baking tray and leave for another hour. Bake in a moderate oven for one hour or until brown.

*Eggs should be thought of as a seasonal food only. So when making this recipe think of it as a springtime treat.

Barley bread with beer

>   500g barley flour
>   500g stone-ground wheat flour
>   1 tsp salt
>   250g butter
>   Beer to mix

Mix the flours and salt together and rub in the butter. Add enough beer to make a soft dough and shape into small cakes. Cook on a hot griddle until firm. This is a very light bread because of the addition of the beer and is very good with cheese.

Autumn fruit bread

>1 kg stone-ground flour
>1 bowl of blackberries (*Rubus fruticosus*)
>1 tsp salt
>500g honey
>Water to mix

Mix the flour with the blackberries then add the honey and water. Shape into small cakes and cook on a griddle, or make two loaves and bake in an oven for one hour.

Fresh fruit yeasted bread

>1.5kg stone-ground flour
>1 bowl fresh elderberries (*Sambucus*)
>500g honey
>1 tsp salt
>Water to mix

Mix all the ingredients together and leave in a warm place for three hours. Knead and shape into two loaves and leave on a tray for another two hours. Bake in a moderate oven for one hour. Serve with butter. This is a yeasted bread because of the natural wild yeast that lives on the elderberries.

In one of the ancient Irish texts about the Feast of Bricriu, it is related that, 'He gathered food for a whole year, and he built a house at Dun Rudraige from which to serve it.' There is a list of the food that was prepared for this monumental feast; the last part of the menu was: '100 wheaten loaves baked in honey'. It seemed strange to me that this particular quotation did not describe 100 wheaten loaves with honey, or 100 wheaten honey loaves. It described loaves baked in honey. At an open-air cooking demonstration, I decided to try this wheaten loaf baked in honey in a stone bank oven. This is an oven that is cut into an earthen bank and lined with large granite stones. A small hole is left at the back of the oven to allow the smoke to escape when a fire is lit inside. After a fire has been roaring for about an hour in the oven, the ashes are brushed out and a bowl containing the bread floating in honey was put into it. The dough I used was the rich fruit bread recipe. I poured a litre of runny honey into a ceramic bowl and dropped the dough into this in one piece. I have to say that I was convinced that the honey would burn when it was put into this very hot

53 Sweet fruit bread baked in honey

oven. However, the stone was placed to seal the oven and grass turf was placed on the cracks to seal the heat in. After two hours the oven door was opened and, to my amazement, the bread was cooked to perfection. The honey was not burnt at all and had partly seeped into the bread dough, making a delightfully sticky prehistoric equivalent to a rum baba without the rum. The waiting crowd — a party from a French archaeological society — devoured the whole loaf in a matter of minutes, breaking pieces off with their fingers and licking them with delight afterwards. I was very pleased with this reaction as the French are thought to be people of great discernment when it comes to food. This recipe is well worth trying but, be warned, is also very sticky. Try it with any of the sweet bread doughs and make it in a conventional oven if you do not have the time to construct a bank oven. Just pour a few pounds of honey into a bowl and float the bread dough on top. This recipe is now an established item on the menu, whenever I give a prehistoric cooking demonstration.

7 Dairy food

There is little doubt that dairy foods were an important part of the prehistoric diet in northern Europe from as early as Neolithic times. Andrew Sherratt discusses the usefulness of milk as an addition to any diet, but looks on it as a secondary use of draught animals (as mentioned in the last chapter):

> Milk has several advantages. From a dietary point of view, it supplies the amino-acid lysine, which is missing in a cereal-based food. It contains fat, protein and sugar in a balanced form and is a useful source of calcium. Being liquid it is easily handled, and can be converted into a variety of storable products.

Archaeology now has evidence that milk products were consumed throughout Europe from Neolithic times due to a new testing technique developed by researchers at Bristol University. They have developed a technique for recognising particular dairy-based fats preserved in Neolithic pottery vessels. A high proportion of the bones excavated at many causeway camps in southern Britain were of calves. The cattle bones from Hambledon Hill are primarily those of older females and young calves. One archaeologist has interpreted these as the kill residue from a dairy herd kept in the settlement. This implies not just the consumption of veal, but the need for a large supply of milk for the community. The management of cattle herds continued through the Bronze Age and, in some ways, took on a ritual significance at various burial mounds. Perhaps the number of cattle consumed at the burial feast was an indication of a person's prestige and wealth, displayed by covering the tomb with the heads of the cattle. Archaeologists excavated 184 cattle skulls at one of these mounds.

Strabo tells us that hides were one of the trade goods exported to Europe from Britain prior to the Roman invasion; he states

> [Britain] bears grain, cattle, gold, silver, and iron. These things are exported from the island as also hides, slaves, and dogs.

Dairy food

21 A bucket of bog butter from the store of the Royal Cornwall Museum

He also comments on the cattle in Britain when he talks about the inhabitants of the Cassiderides — thought to be the Scilly Isles and Cornwall:

> They live off their herds . . . As they have mines of tin and lead, they give these metals and the hides from their cattle to the sea traders.

These quotations support the conclusion that large herds of cattle were a common sight in ancient Britain. Milk would have been available all year round due to good animal husbandry, although the milk would have been more sweet, rich and plentiful in the spring. So the storing of surplus dairy produce would have been important to such a culture, as supplies of milk would decrease during the winter months. This problem was overcome — in part — by storing butter in wooden containers and burying them in marshlands or peat bogs. Deep in the peat levels of the marsh, the surplus butter would keep fresh during the summer months, only to be removed when required during the winter. Archaeologists in Ireland have discovered large quantities of this 'bog butter'; the discoveries range in quantity from a few pounds to as much as a hundredweight. I have held a wooden stave bucket containing at least 5kg of ancient butter from the Royal Cornwall Museum store, in Truro (**21**). A Mr. H. Maulslay found this butter in the neighbourhood of Ougherard, County Galway in 1906; he reported, 'This cask containing Irish butter was found when turf was being cut five feet below the surface in solid peat.' It is a pale yellow in colour, has a grainy consistency and smells quite dreadful, although it is fascinating to think that this particular bucket-full of rancid butter was churned by someone in Ireland possibly a couple of thousand years ago, when the map of Europe was dominated by the Roman legions. The northern European taste for butter is still with us, no matter how many health warnings there may be about its consumption. We have had a tradition of eating butter for possibly 6000 years — since the Neolithic times — so it is not surprising that it is a habit we find hard to rid ourselves of. Strabo thought it warranted mentioning that the Celtiberians ate butter instead of olive oil with their bread, even though they had access to olive oil in the south of Spain: '. . . instead of olive oil they use butter'.

However, bogs are not a good environment for storing hard cheeses, which would have been an important source of protein and calcium in people's diet in the winter months. Hard cheese needs a suitable place to store as it matures, somewhere cool and dark. In prehistory the obvious place to store cheese for the winter months would have been in caves. Not only does a cave store the cheese perfectly, but it can also impart flavour to the cheese in the form of localised moulds that live in the cave. Cheeses made of ewe's milk, such as Roquefort from France, are said to acquire their unique flavour from such moulds in the caves of that region. In Britain the famous Cheddar cheese was developed in the caves of Cheddar Gorge, where the extensive caves were used to store and mature this cheese.

22 *A picture of the fogou at Carn Euny: a good place in which to have matured cheeses*

However, caves are not a widespread feature in the northern European landscape. The man-made underground structure, known as a 'fogou' in Cornwall (**22**) or 'souterrain', found in several parts of Britain, could have been constructed partly for this purpose as well as for the storage of wines and meads. As many as 200 examples of souterrains have been discovered in Scotland, dating from the first century BC to the third century AD. On Orkney and Shetland they are built entirely underground, yet in eastern Scotland they are only partly subterranean. It is possible however that not all British prehistoric tribes made cheese. The writer Strabo says about the British, 'some of them although well supplied with milk make no cheese'. This might account for the lack of these archaeological features in some parts of Britain. Tacitus the Roman writer, when describing the Germans, mentions underground stores such as fogous and souterrains:

> They have also the habit of hollowing out caves underground and heaping masses of refuse on the top. In these they can escape the winter's cold and store their produce.

This suggests that the practice of making artificial caves for food storage was widespread in Europe. Dairy production must have had quite an effect on prehistoric societies: ceramics had to be developed to store and strain the milk during cheese- and butter-making processes, storage facilities were needed to preserve surplus butter for the winter months, and underground caves sought or made to mature the cheese. Also, the size of a family's herd could have become a status symbol, shown by the number of cattle that could be consumed at a burial and the leaving of cattle heads as a testimony to this status. Pliny, when talking about the Celts said they considered butter as their favourite accompaniment to food, '... the one thing that distinguishes the wealthy man from the lower orders'. Cream would probably have been clotted, as it is today in the west country, to prolong its keeping qualities. So I will start this section with a simple recipe for making clotted cream.

Clotted cream

You will need a large shallow pan; an enamel roasting tin for example.

Method no 1 (using whole milk)

Leave the milk in the tin in a cool place for a day until the cream rises to the top.

Dairy food

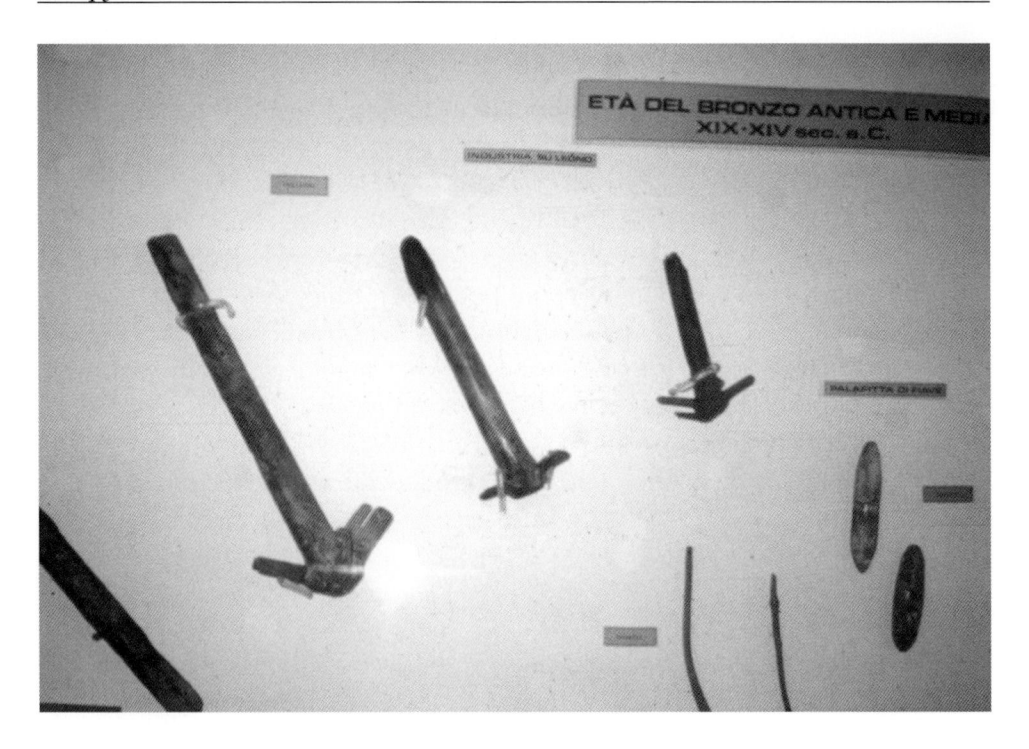

23 Sticks used to whisk cream into butter found at Lake Ledro in Northern Italy; very similar sticks have also been found a Flag Fen in Britain. The author has used copies of this type of stick for making butter and found them very effective

Carefully carry the tin to the cooker, heat very slowly until a skin forms on the top and begins to wrinkle the surface. Remove from the heat and leave until cold. Carefully skim off the clotted cream the next day.

Method No 2 (using cream)

Place the cream in a heatproof dish, into a tin filled with water and place directly onto the heat. Bring the water to the boil, then simmer for 20 minutes until the cream is scalded and a crust is formed on the top. Allow to cool overnight and skim off the clotted cream as above.

Butter

There are a few methods for making butter using whole milk and butter churns. The milk is left in the churn to ripen, then agitated until the butter floats to the top — hot stones heated in the fire can be added to speed up the separation. The making of butter is a fascinating process to watch, although we all take it for granted today. The best method is to start with double cream.

You will need a whisk (**23**), a bowl, a strainer, a small piece of butter-muslin or loose-weave cloth and two wooden spoons. To truly re-enact the prehistoric process, try to make the whisk first from some green hazel or willow sticks. To begin with strip the bark off the sticks with a knife. If this is done in the spring the bark will strip off in one piece as the sap is rising in the plant at that time of year — keep this bark for binding the whisk together. Then very carefully bend three of the sticks and secure them all at the cut end with the strips of bark or string. You have now made a very effective balloon whisk with which to make butter (**24, 25 & 26**).

Butter-making

Stage 1: Pour about 450g of the double cream into a bowl and begin to whisk. Continue until it is as stiff as you would use to fill a cake.

Stage 2: Keep on whisking until the cream looks like scrambled eggs and starts to look grainy in texture.

Stage 3: Now it becomes very hard to whisk and your stick whisk is put to the test. The mixture starts to make a watery noise. You will know what I mean, as you hear it, it is quite difficult to describe but very noticeable. The butter becomes yellow as it starts to separate itself from the buttermilk and at this stage the yellow butter forms a solid lump in the middle of the white buttermilk liquid.

Stage 4: Strain and save the buttermilk, perhaps to make some pancakes or sweet bread. The butter has to be washed with lots of fresh water to remove all of the buttermilk, otherwise the butter will go rancid very quickly. If the butter is to be consumed that day, then this is not so important. The best way to wash it is to put it back into the bowl and stir with the spoon, adding fresh water every now and then, and straining. Continue until the water runs clear.

Stage 5: Add a little salt to the butter and, with the two wooden spoons, squeeze small pieces of butter extracting as much water as possible and put it onto a plate. The butter is now ready to use.

Dairy food

24 The first stage of butter making after making the stick balloon whisk

25 The second stage of butter making, when the buttermilk separates from the butter

26 The third stage of butter making, when the butter is strained through a nettle fibre cloth and a rush strainer and is ready to be washed and salted

Soft cheese

There are many simple methods of cheese-making still being practised around Europe. These simple methods would doubtless have been used in prehistoric times too. Here are a few recipes to make soft cheeses to add to your prehistoric meal.

Sour cream cheese

> 1 litre whole milk
> 250ml of sour cream (This can be fresh cream that has been left in a warm place for a few days, or perhaps the cream that can often be bought at a supermarket at a reduced price)
> A piece of butter-muslin or loose-weave cloth and string

Put the milk in a pan and slowly bring to the boil. Remove from the heat. Add to this the sour cream and stir, the curd will separate from the whey as you stir it. Place in the cloth to strain and tie the top of the cloth to form a bag with the curds in it. Hang this bag of curds from a hook over a bowl and allow to drip for at least one hour. Empty the contents of the bag into a bowl, add a little salt and you have soft cheese. This can then be flavoured (See the possible flavourings at the end of this section).

Vinegar cheese

>1 litre whole milk
>28ml of wine vinegar
>A strainer cloth and string as before.

This is a very simple and economic cheese to make. It can be made just as well with either goats' or cows' milk. Put the milk into a pan and slowly bring to the boil. When the milk is just starting to rise in the pan, turn off the heat, add the vinegar and stir. Keep stirring until the curds and whey separate — this usually happens almost immediately. Strain as above and add a little salt before use.

Beer cheese

>1 litre whole milk
>250ml good beer
>strainer cloth and string

The method is just the same as the others, but uses beer instead of sour cream or vinegar. The addition of the beer gives enough acidity to separate the curds. This cheese has a very beery taste to it and goes very well with barley bread and butter.

Smoked soft cheese

To make a smoked cheese, follow any of the above soft cheese methods but keep the cheese in the muslin bag after it has been strained. When the cheese has hung for at least 24 hours and is quite firm to the touch, hang it high up over a wood fire so that it does not get too hot but is enveloped in cool smoke. Oak wood or apple wood is best for this method. After four hours, the smoked cheese can be put on a plate and left to cool before use. A soft smoked cheese similar to this is still eaten in Denmark today.

27 Nettle leaf covered cheese, still made in Cornwall today

Storing soft cheese

Once the curd has been strained for 24 hours it can be taken out of the cloth and stored in a brine solution until needed. This is a very good way of keeping it. A traditional method used in Britain was to bury the cheese in the ground for a few days to improve the flavour. Take the cheese out of the cloth and wrap in either blanched hazel leaves (*Corylus avellana*) or blanched nettle leaves (*Urtica dioica*) (**27**). Place this into a pot or box, seal with a lid and leave to mature. This makes for a very nice cheese with a unique flavour.

Cheese flavouring

Savoury flavouring of cheese can be achieved by simply adding various wild herbs, such as wild chives (*Allium schoenoprasum*), marjoram (*Origanum vulgare*), myrtle (*Myrica gale*) (**28**), thyme (*Acinos arvensis*), mint (*Mentha*); or any wild berry, such as blackberry (*Rubus fruticosus*), bilberry (*Vaccinium myrtillus/uliginosum*), raspberry (*Rubus idaeus*) or wild strawberry (*Fragaria vesca*).

28 A basket made from Bog Myrtle for keeping soft cheese in. It not only flavours the cheese but also keeps flies away from the contents

Roasted hazelnuts are a good addition to any of the savoury or sweet cheeses. A combination of honey and roasted hazelnuts is good too. Honey alone can also be added to the cheese.

These types of cheeses and various flavourings would have been made only for special occasions, such as festivals, or maybe at times of plenty. They are very simple to make and compliment the bread recipes beautifully.

Hard cheese

To make a hard cheese that can be stored over the winter is a longer process which requires a lot of equipment and space. The curd is set with the enzyme from a calf's stomach — now known as rennet — and the set curd is then cut and drained several times. The next part of the process is to put the curd into a mould and apply weights to press it. After varying times under weights, and changing the muslin cloths at each stage, the hard cheese, is covered with fresh dry cloths. Sometimes wax or pig fat is applied to this to seal the cheese. The cheese now needs a suitable place to store in order to mature. This must be a cool and dark place, like a cave as mentioned at the beginning of this chapter.

8 Meat, fish and vegetable stews

The convenience of cooking a meal in one pot must have been as obvious to our prehistoric ancestors as it is today. The recipes that follow are not the kind of meal that would have been made on a hunting expedition, but rather the sort of meal that could have been made in a settlement. They may have been made with scraps of meat after butchering an animal, or they may have been used to cook tough meat that needed a longer cooking time. I will look at the kind of foods that hunters might have eaten in the next chapter. The archaeological evidence for meat-eating is strong — witness the large quantities of bone remains found in prehistoric rubbish dumps. In addition, the comments made by most classical historians about the Celts indicate that meat was the staple of their diet. Athenaeus says, 'Their food consists of a few loaves of bread, but large quantities of meat'. Still, it is quite possible that some did not eat meat and it is interesting to consider an alternative diet for them. There are also an increasing number of vegetarians in our society today, so I have created some meatless alternatives for most of these recipes.

Here is a recipe that could be made for a festival or fundraiser, it is very simple to make and always popular with the carnivores that I have tried it on.

Lamb stew (for a party of 45 people) (**colour plate 10**)

> 1.5kg chopped or minced lamb
> 1kg leeks — as an alternative to the wild onion ramsons (*Allium ursinum*)
> 1 good bunch of sorrel
> 1 bunch of chickweed (*Stellaria media*)
> 2 bunches of chives
> 3kg peas
> 2 large sprigs of mint
> 4 tsp salt
> 2kg bulgar wheat (this is chopped, pre-cooked and dried wheat)

Fry the lamb in a large pan until browned, there should be enough fat in the lamb without having to add any more. Add the chopped sorrel, chives, leeks and chickweed and cook until tender. Add the peas, mint, salt and enough water to cover it. Simmer for approximately 30 minutes. Add the bulgar wheat and simmer until all the stock has been absorbed. Serve preferably in wooden bowls and eat at once.

Vegetable stew (for 15 people)

125g hazelnuts
100g butter
1 bunch of sorrel
1 bunch of chives and wild marjoram
1kg chopped leeks
1kg peas
1 sprig of mint
750g bulgar wheat
2 tsps salt

Fry the nuts (chopped) in the butter for five minutes. Add the chopped leeks and herbs, except the mint, and cook until soft. Add the peas, mint and salt and cover with water. Simmer for 30 minutes. Add the bulgar wheat and cook until all the stock is absorbed. Serve at once, this is a very tasty stew and could have been made in the springtime to use up the hazelnuts from the winter store.

Mutton stew

One loin of mutton cut into pieces (or lamb if not available)
2 tbs of stone-ground flour
28g butter
2 tsp salt
28g mustard seeds
Water

Dust the mutton with the flour and salt and fry in the butter until brown. Add the mustard seed and cover with water. This can be cooked in an earthenware casserole dish with a lid. Mix a little flour and water in a bowl and use it to glue the lid to the dish; this makes an airtight seal. If you have an old pot it is better if, once sealed, it is placed at the edge of an open fire. Alternatively, it can be cooked in an oven for three hours. There is nothing quite so tasty, as eating a bowl of mutton stew with large chunks of bread out in the open. I would recommend it to those who are tired of conventional barbecue evenings.

Rich mutton stew with juniper berries

    1kg chopped mutton
    A piece of butter for frying
    4 whole ramson plants, leaves and bulbs (or use onion)
    1 litre of dry red wine
    10 juniper berries
    1 tsp salt
    A piece of butter for frying

Fry the meat in a very hot pan with the butter. Add the chopped onion or ramsons then add the red wine, juniper berries and salt. Put into a pot and seal with a flour paste and lid. Place in an oven or by a fire for at least four hours. The rich aroma of this dish is wonderful. Serve in bowls with chunks of bread to soak up the gravy.

Pigeon stew

    2 prepared pigeons
    28g lard
    1 sprig of marjoram and myrtle
    1 bunch of chives
    1 handful of sorrel
    1 tsp salt
    1 pint of blackberry wine (or dry red wine)
    1 pint water

Fry the pigeons (cut into two) in the lard until brown and add the salt and herbs. Cover with the wine and water and simmer in a sealed pot (as above) for one and a half hours until tender.

The bones of pigeons were found in prehistoric middens at Glastonbury Iron Age lake village settlement in the west of England. There is a surprisingly amount of breast meat on even a small pigeon.

Hare stew

    250g streaky bacon
    25g butter
    1 hare that has been hung (or a rabbit)
    1 bunch of chives
    lkg chopped parsnip (there is a wild parsnip, but it can be confused with some very poisonous members of the umbellifer family of plants, so I suggest using cultivated parsnips for this recipe to be on the safe side)
    1 tsp salt
    Water

Fry the bacon in the butter in a pan slowly to release the fat, then add the hare or rabbit joints. Cook until golden brown. Add the chives, salt, the parsnips and enough water to cover. Simmer for 1 hour over a stove or in a sealed pot as before. The parsnips caramelise and thicken the stock in this recipe. Very tasty, but be careful of the bones as they can be quite small.

Pork and beer stew

There is a wealth of quotations by the classical historians that the Celts in Europe loved wine and beer. Athenaeus mentions that 'the wheat beer prepared with honey, in Gaul was drunk by the poorer classes'. A lot of old country recipes also include beer, mainly to tenderise rather tough cuts of meat. Here are two for you to try. The tougher cuts of meat tended to be from older animals which, although they do take longer to cook, have much more flavour than young animals.

    1 loin of pork
    28g lard
    1 cooking apple or 5 chopped crab apples
    1 bunch of chives
    500g peas
    1 tsp salt
    1 pint brown ale

Brown the pork in the pan with the lard. Add the chopped apples, chives, salt and peas, and cover with the beer. Seal in a pot or simmer slowly over the stove for two hours until the meat is tender. Serve with chunks of bread to soak up the gravy.

Beef and beer stew

>500g stewing steak
>28g wholemeal flour
>28g butter
>1 tsp salt
>1 large bunch of sorrel
>56g honey
>1 pint of brown ale

Dust the meat in flour and fry in the butter until brown. Add the salt and chopped herbs. Then add the honey and beer and seal in a pot. Cook for one and a half hours until tender. Serve, as before, with bread.

Bass stew with wild mushrooms

>125g fatty bacon
>1 bunch of chives
>1 sprig of myrtle
>1 bowl of wild field mushrooms (*Agarius campestris*)*
>1 large filleted fish
>1 litre white wine
>1 litre water
>1 tsp salt

Fry the bacon in small pieces with all the chopped herbs. When soft, add the chopped mushrooms and cook for a few minutes. Cut the fish fillets into pieces and put into the pot with the wine, water and salt. Simmer over a low heat for one hour.

* A note of caution: please be careful when gathering wild mushrooms, unless you know how to recognise them. Many wild varieties of mushrooms can now be bought from supermarkets. I am sure that mushrooms would have been eaten in prehistoric times, and also possibly dried for winter use.

Cod and oysters in beer

    3 ramson plants or 3 onions
    1 bowlful of fresh spring beech leaves (or use cabbage leaves)
    1 large piece of butter
    1kg cod
    250g oysters
    1 litre brown ale
    1 litre water
    1 tsp salt
    40ml vinegar
    1 spring of myrtle
    Chunks of wholemeal bread chopped into cubes

Fry the beech leaves and ramsons (or onions) in a pot with butter until soft. Cut the cod into pieces and add to the pot along with the oysters. Cover with the beer, water, vinegar and salt. Drop in the sprig of myrtle. Seal the pot with a lid and some flour paste. Cook by the fire for at least two hours. Add the cubed bread — this soaks up the stock and thickens it. Eat immediately.

Soused fish in wine

Any fish can be cooked in this manner, although we only tend to cook herrings this way nowadays. Put some fish in a pot, add some mustard seed and some salt to taste. Cover with a mixture of water and white wine. Seal the pot and cook by the fire for one hour.

Rollmops

This simple method for pickling fish must have originated in ancient times to preserve the catch. Any fish can be pickled in this way, even salmon which tastes very good. Roll fish fillets with a ramson bulb or small onion inside. Place into a pot and add some mustard seeds and a little grated horseradish. Cover with white wine vinegar and leave for at least a week. The fish tastes good up to a month stored in this way. If stored longer, the fish meat still tastes good but becomes very soft.

Smoked fish stew (colour plates 15 & 20)

125g bacon
2 leeks
500g of any smoked fish
1 litre milk
1 cup of cream
Some chives
1 tsp salt

Fry the bacon until the fat comes away from it and add the chopped leeks. Cook until tender. Add the fillets of fish and cover with the milk. Slowly cook in a pot near the fire until the fish is cooked, which about 30 minutes. Pour in the cream, along with the chopped chives and salt. This is very good eaten with simple oat bread.

Cod with mustard sauce (a traditional Scottish recipe)

1 bunch of chives
1kg fresh cod
1 cup milk
1 cup water
A little salt
3 tbs butter
2 tbs flour
1 handful of crushed mustard seeds

Put the fish into a pan on top of the chives (this stops it from sticking). Add the milk and water and salt and simmer gently for 10 minutes. Remove the fish and chives and keep warm by the fire. Melt the butter in a pan and stir in the flour and mustard seeds. Add the fish liquor and stir until it thickens. Pour over the fish and eat at once.

9 Cooking with hot stones

Hunting food

This is the type of food that prehistoric people could have eaten while away from home on a hunting expedition. The classical Historian Herodotus described the hunting practices of the Sythian people in 450 BC. These people lived a nomadic life on the steppes, a vast belt of grassland stretching from Manchuria in the east to European Russia in the west. I am including it in the book because I find this description of resourcefulness fascinating — I am sure you will too. I am also convinced that this type of adaptability to the landscape would have been relevant to all their European prehistoric counterparts. Herodotus writes:

> Now the Sythian land is wonderous bare of wood: so this is their device for the cooking of flesh. When they have flayed the victims, they strip the flesh from the bones and throw it into the cauldrons of the country, if they have such: into these they throw the flesh, and cook it by lighting a fire beneath with the bones of the victims. But if they have no cauldron, then they cast all the flesh into the victim's stomachs, adding water thereto, and make a fire beneath of the bones, which burn finely; the stomachs easily hold the flesh when it is stripped from the bones; thus a ox serves to cook itself, and every other victim does likewise.

Quite a description, I think, of how ancient people made nature work for them; not just using the stomach of the animal for a pot to cook itself in, but making a fire out of the bones where there was a shortage of wood.

There is an example of this type of self-sufficiency in the lives of the Siriono tribe of Bolivia today. Here is a quotation from *The Anthropologists Cookbook* by A. Holuberg.

> Little care is taken in dressing game, which is done either by men or women. Animals with hair, such as monkeys and peccaries, are first singed whole in the fire, and the burnt hair is then scraped off with

the fingernails or with a small section of a midrib of a motacu palm leaf. The animal is then gutted with a sharp piece of bamboo, after which the whole carcass is sometimes (but by no means always) perfunctorily washed before it is cooked. Birds are hastily plucked and then singed in the fire and gutted. If an animal is small it is usually cooked whole, but if it is too large for a pot (or too large to roast rapidly) it is quartered or cut up into smaller pieces with a bamboo knife. Armoured animals like the armadillo and tortoise are usually thrown in the fire and left there to roast in their shells.

This insight into the practices of the Siriono people today is, I feel, comparable to the way the Sythian people in Herodotus' time used the natural resources available to them to prepare and cook their quarry. The minimum of effort is the pivot around which the hunter-gatherer cultures of past and present function. The need to travel light on a hunting expedition would have been fundamental as the carcass of the quarry would have to be carried home to camp. Therefore, a makeshift cooking pot or utensil would have been needed to cook meals while travelling away from home.

Pot boilers

Typical features of prehistoric settlements in Cornwall are piles of small round pebbles, thought to be either for sling shot use or as pot boilers. I have conducted a great deal of research into the uses of these small stones in cooking and have found them to be surprisingly efficient. Once I put a layer of small beach stones on the ground and lit a fire on top of them. On this particular occasion I was researching possible soft cheese-making techniques using pot boilers. A large pot was placed on a low table a few metres away from the fire. Into this pot was poured one litre of whole milk and a small bowl of sour cream to increase the acidity and help separate the curds and whey. With the use of a pair of hazel stick tongs, five stones were dropped into the milk. The stones do not tend to release their heat immediately but the milk began to steam after a few minutes. More stones were added — three in all — and the milk began to boil. Almost immediately, the curds separated from the whey, which was subsequently strained through some rushes and the soft cheese remained (**29**). The practicability of using hot stones to heat the contents of cooking pots becomes immediately apparent. This especially if one has had some experience of stirring pots of food over smoky fires. Food can be prepared at some distance from the fire leaving a space for people to either warm themselves, or spit roast some meat. All that is needed to keep many

1 The type of marshy landscape the Mesolithic people would have known

2 The remains of a Bronze Age lake settlement at Lake Ledro in northern Italy

3   A Beaker Pot from the Royal Cornwall Museum

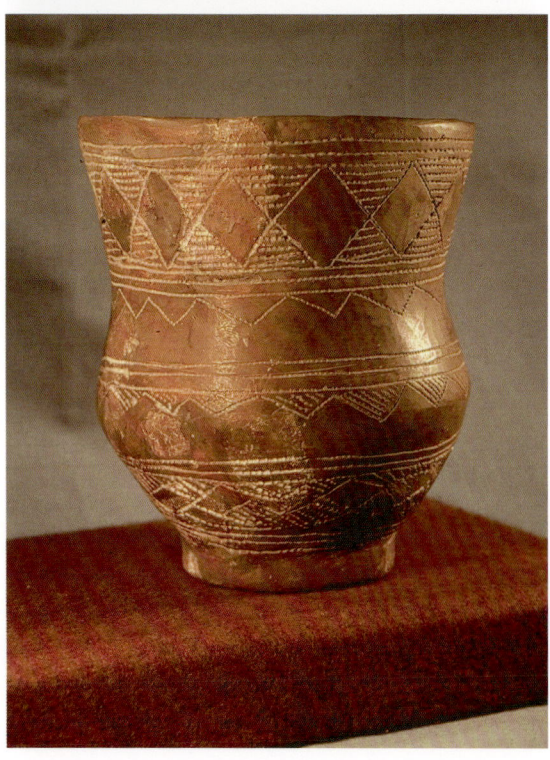

4   Another Beaker Pot, but without the handle, from the same museum

5   A gold lunulae *from the Royal Cornwall museum*

6   Modern day St Michael's Mount island that is thought to have been the island Strabo mentions in his description of the Cornish tin trade

7 *An example of a Baltic boat to carry trade in northern Europe in prehistoric times*

8 *A typical Bronze age round house (one of the author's houses at her research establishment)*

9   Two Lithuanian women making copies of Lime bark buckets at Biskupin in Poland

10 The lamb stew from page 87. The mat under the bowl is made from Flag Iris leaves

11 Examples of typical textiles from Iron Age Europe

12 Querning grain into flour at the Romano-British settlement of Chysauster, where the author ran ancient technology camps for schoolchildren

13 A large clome bread oven being demonstrated at Biskupin in Poland

14 One of the author's rare breed sheep. It is a Manx Loughton, the type of sheep kept in prehistory. The bones of these sheep are thicker than the modern varieties and make good bone needles

15 *The smoked fish stew from page 93. The smoked fish next to the stew are, from the top, herring, trout and mackerel*

16 *After four hours the meat is ready to eat. The dough casing is turned upside down and the soft base cut away to reveal the cooked meat. This example is the honey-covered ham mentioned on page 99*

17 *A picture of the King Carp stuffed with plums from page 113*

18 The barred of salted pilchards described on page 120

19 Some winkles used in the winkle butter recipe on page 123

20 Some fish being smoked over a hot fire. The frame, sticks and string are all made from a single branch of willow

21 The sweet bean cakes from pages 130 and 173

22 *A picture of ramsons (page 149) — very easy to identify as you smell the strong oniony odour before actually seeing the plant!*

23 *Some wild Spring salad ingredients: gorse flowers, primrose flowers, violet flowers, chives, Jack-by-the-hedge, hawthorn leaves and sheep's sorrel*

24 The familiar gorse flowers are very tasty in a wild salad

25 Jack-by-the-hedge (page 153), only found in springtime

26 Elderberries

27 *A bowl of blackberries and peas for their autumn harvest (pge 127)*

29 A pot with milk into which hot stones have been placed to make soft cheese

different pots simmering is the addition every so often of a few firestones. As the stones cool in the pots they can be thrown back into the fire for re-heating. This technique was also used in Hawaii but, instead of dropping hot stones into a ceramic pot, a calabash (a hollowed out gourd shell), was used as the container. Fish was thought to be delicious by the Hawaiian islanders when cooked in a calabash with hot stones.

Bread stones

At Lake Ledro in northern Italy another interesting cooking technique was found in the archaeology. A loaf looking like a large doughnut, made from a flour of coarsely-ground cereals, was discovered. It is suggested that the dough had been wrapped around a previously heated stone that was found at the site. I found another example of this type of bread-cooking method in Britain. Archaeologists at the Iron Age settlement of Glastonbury found an almost identical doughnut-shaped piece of bread that had been cooked on a stone. Eager to try this out, I made a coarse grain dough, found a granite stone about the same size as the ones in Italy and Glastonbury and heated the stone until it was red hot. I sprinkled the stone with flour and it vaporised. So I thought I would just place the piece of bread dough on the stone and see what happened — it immediately smelt like burnt toast. However, I decided to leave it on the stone for about two hours, which is the time it takes to lose all the heat from the granite stone. Amazingly enough, the bread pulled away from the stone quite easily and was cooked very well apart from a thin crust that was in direct contact with the stone. Possibly this was a method used to slowly cook some bread over the morning or afternoon while out working so that the bread was ready to eat on returning home. This type of coarse-floured bread is best eaten when fresh or it becomes too dry and hard to eat. So maybe this slow stone-cooking method solved this problem for those who had not the patience to grind their flour completely.

Stone pits or earth ovens

The efficiency of the earth oven as a cooking technique must have occurred to primitive cultures on a global scale. Not only does this method leave the community free from work for four or five hours but it also saves considerable amounts of fuel. A number of pits were discovered at an excavation of Bronze Age cairns at Stannon on Bodmin Moor. Cairn one exposed at its centre a pit that had been dug into the subsoil to a depth of 35cm; the pit was round and 1m in diameter. Its sides sloped to the bottom, rather like a cauldron, and it was lined with small stones. The bottom of the pit contained large carbonised chunks of wood which were reasonably preserved due to the wet conditions. This pit had been carefully back-filled with soil, a flat stone had been placed on top, and eight stones were placed around the edge. These acted as supports for eight larger stones which were placed leaning against them. This was repeated several times in what appeared to be a spiral pattern. Over this structure was piled a large number of small moorland stones. In cairn two there were two pits, one long and rectangular and the other a small round pit next to it. The rectangular pit was filled with soil and the small round one contained traces of charcoal. However, between these two pits was a piece of soft, shapeless, lightly fired clay. The third pit was a typical cairn burial containing a decorated funerary urn. This suggests that, as only one cairn contained a burial, the other two were in some way part of a ceremony connected with it. This is especially true of cairn one, which was very carefully covered by a flat stone supporting the petal-like structure of stones on top. It is possible that some sort of wake meal was consumed at the burial. The small fragment of soft clay found between the two pits in cairn two suggests that some food might have been baked in it, as it was not comparable to any typical ceramic find. One would have expected quite a considerable amount of this partly fired clay if this were the case.

It is difficult to suggest why there was only one piece; maybe the relations took home a piece of the clay from the deceased's wake as a memento of their farewell meal. This is pure conjecture, but plausible as a hypothesis. Ceremonial earth ovens associated with funerals are well documented by anthropologists studying the Maori peoples of New Zealand and in Polynesia. In the Maori *whakau* ceremony, the oven was large enough to cook a meal for the entire funeral party. On Tikopia Island in Polynesia, the earth oven was also used and is described as being a pit in the ground in which food is cooked by being laid on hot stones and covered with leaves. I have reconstructed the Stannon cairn one pit and found the cauldron shape had a spectacular effect on the ferocity of the fire within it — this being due to the smooth airflow in and out of the pit. When reconstructing this pit, it became apparent that the stone lining was there for a specific purpose, looking very similar to the earth oven bases of Polynesia. The fire can be lit directly on top of the stones in the pit and a second hearth nearby can heat the other half of the stones needed to be put on top of the food to be cooked. In addition to this turf sods are placed over the top layer of stones to keep the heat in until the food is cooked.

During my experiments, I found that the free-flowing air in the pit induces such a fierce fire that the stone lining of the pit becomes red hot in one hour instead of two hours which is the time it takes to heat the stone lining of a square pit. During one experiment a joint of beef was smeared with mustard seed paste and salt, wrapped in a simple flour and water dough, and then dropped into the pit. Stones from a second hearth were added over the top and turf was layered on this to keep the heat in. After four hours the bread-covered meat was taken out. The top of the dough casing was so hard it could have been used as battle armour, although the dough underneath was soft and palatable. If the dough is immediately turned upside down when it is taken out of the pit, the hard top crust acts as a bowl to contain the wonderful gravy that had formed inside the dough casing. The meat inside the bread bowl was consistently, perfectly cooked and surrounded by this pool of rich gravy. On other occasions I have tried different meats such as a large ham that I covered with a thick layer of honey before covering it with the dough. This was undoubtedly the best honey baked ham I have tasted and is highly recommended if you want to experiment with stone pit cooking. At cooking demonstrations, this ham and the beef in gravy is usually devoured by the crowd in minutes, so make sure you use a large joint of meat when you try it (**30, 31, 32, 33, colour plate 16, & 34**).

30 The beef will be wrapped in the bread dough, before being put in the stone pit to cook

31 Here the granite stones are being heated to put on top of the pit

32 The bread-wrapped beef is now in the pit and is being covered with hot stones

33 A mat and then soil cover the stones to keep the heat in

34 Two of the previous day's bread casings, so hard-baked that they are not even eaten by birds or the dogs and cats at the Biskupin centre

Water pits

When looking into the subject of prehistoric hunting foods and cooking methods, it is essential that something is said about 'burnt mound archaeology'; this is the term for the excavation in many parts of Europe of large piles of fire-cracked stones, hence the term 'burnt mound'. Associated with these excavations are large water-tight troughs; it is believed that stones were heated in a fire, then dropped into the water trough. The purpose of this is thought to be for the cooking of joints of meat in the water. Professor Michael O'Kelly from Ireland built a reconstruction of a water trough that he excavated at Ballyvourney, County Cork in 1954. He cooked a 5kg leg of mutton in this trough by adding heated stones, it took 3 hours 40 minutes to cook the mutton to perfection. Burnt mounds (or *fulachta fiadh* as they are called in Ireland) have been traditionally viewed as field kitchens or base camps for roving hunters. Early Irish literature seems to support this view — *The History of Ireland*, written in 1908 by G. Keating says

> [It] was their custom to send their attendants about noon with whatever they had killed in the morning's hunt to an appointed hill,

having wood and moorland in the neighbourhood, and to kindle raging fires thereon, and put into them a large number of emery stones; and to dig two pits in the yellow clay of the moorland, and put some of the meat on spits to roast before the fire; and then bind another portion of it with sugans (grasses) in dry bundles, and set it to boil in the larger of the two pits, and keep plying them with stones that were in the fire, making them seethe often until they were cooked. And these fires were so large that their sites are today in Ireland burnt to blackness and these are now called Fulacht Fian (or Cooking Places) by the peasantry.

A conference in Ireland in 1990 highlighted the fact that these types of sites contain fire-cracked stones from the Bronze Age period. They are typical in other parts of Europe as well as the British Isles. A water pit and mound of fire-cracked stones was found at the site of an ancient stream in the middle of a park called Cob Lane, in Birmingham in 1980. In Sweden they are called Skarvstenshogar, the main distribution of these Bronze Age sites being in eastern parts of central Sweden, in particular the provinces of Vastmanland, Uppland, Sodermanland and Ostergotland. Athenaeus, quoting Posidonius, also mentions the Celts in Europe cooking meat in water:

Their food consists of a few loaves of bread, but large quantities of meat prepared in water or roasted over coals on spits.

This account mirrors the Irish one very well.

Each year I take a team with me to Poland to demonstrate this particular ancient cooking technique, amongst others, at Biskupin — Europe's oldest and most prestigious prehistoric reconstruction (**35**). The site was discovered in a lake area north of Poznan by a schoolteacher before the Second World War. He noticed a large number of stakes on the edge of a lake during a drought year. An excavation followed and it was discovered to be the site of a very large Iron Age lake village, similar to those found in Switzerland and Somerset in Britain. The archaeologists, using local manpower, made a full-size reconstruction of a little of the ramparts and some buildings. The war followed and the Germans did not like this part of Polish history, so they destroyed the reconstruction and most of the excavation reports that they could find. When the war finished it became an important part of Polish pride to reconstruct this part of their prehistoric heritage and a larger reconstruction was built. This reconstruction is now over 50 years old and it was at this centre that I was invited to demonstrate ancient cooking techniques. Biskupin is open all year round, but over the last six years there has been a festival there to celebrate the fortified

35 The famous gatehouse at Biskupin in Poland

36 Some beef ready to be wrapped in grass before being dropped into the water pit

settlement and Polish archaeology in general. The festival lasts nine days and combines education with entertainment. Experimental archaeologists come from all over Europe to demonstrate their skills, such as bronze-casting, iron-smelting, flint-knapping, weaving, pottery and ancient cooking.

Each day a 5kg joint of meat was given to my team to cook in a water pit which was made by burying a half barrel (wooden) in the ground. The joints of meat were merely wrapped in grasses that we picked from the fields each morning and tied with some string. The grass protects the meat from ash and particles of the stones which crumble each time they are re-heated and dropped into the water. The water in the trough has to be brought up to boiling point by adding hot stones for about half an hour before the meat is dropped into it. During the next two hours, we added the odd stone now and then when we notice that the water had stopped bubbling. This is a very popular technique to demonstrate and is quite dramatic to watch. Each time a red hot stone is dropped into the already very hot water, it hisses and spits and makes wonderful gurgling noises. In addition, after about an hour of cooking, the fresh grasses produce a bright lime green colour to the boiling water, reminiscent of a cartoon witches' cauldron. The public usually assume that we are making some strange British soup until the joint of grass-covered meat is pulled out after a few hours (**36 & 37**). After removing the grasses, we then roll

Cooking with hot stones

37 The water pit boiled after fresh hot stones had been dropped in

38 A typical day's cooking at Biskupin festival. Honey-baked ham, carp baked in clay with plums, water pit-bailed beef and sticky honey nut cake

the meat on some hot stones by the fire to crisp up the outside of the joint. Over the nine days of the festival, we cooked 15kg of meat per day and whatever fish the lake fishermen gave us (caught the night before) — we had not one failure. All the meat was cooked and consumed within half an hour of serving it (**38**).

What this shows is that there is no mystery to these primitive methods of cooking food, they are both simple and effective, and it is the easiest and most effective methods that would have been used. It also shows that we appreciate the flavour of primitive cooking just as much, if not more, today than they did then. Having tasted the modern alternative, primitive cooking has a lot to offer, if only as a new, fun way to cook a barbecue. On a long hunting trip, however, a meat-only diet would become tedious so I am sure that prehistoric people would not have wasted the vegetation all about them. A herb pudding could have been added to the pot or water trough that the game was cooked in. All that the hunter would need would be a square of loose woven linen or nettle-fibre cloth, a small bag of oat, barley or wheat flour and a little salt. Various herbs can be chopped, possibly with the liver of the animal caught, then mixed with a little flour and salt and water to bind. This could then be put into a square of cloth, tied into a bundle and dropped into the water pit along with the cooking joint of meat. The meat stock also enhances the flavour of the pudding as it cooks. When the meat is cooked, the pudding would provide not just a type of bread to go with it but also some vegetables.

Here are some pudding recipes; these could also be boiled in plain salted water — to emulate the unfortunate hunter who caught no game that day. These recipes are designed for outdoor campfire cooking, although they could be adapted by boiling the puddings and meat in a large pot over the stove. If hunting game or fishing on the seashore, the herbs for the pudding could be made with seaweeds with the addition of limpets and mussels for a savoury stock.

Nettle pudding no. 1

1 bunch of sorrel (*Rumex acetosa*)
1 bunch of watercress (*Nasturtium officinale*)
1 bunch of dandelion leaves (*Taraxacum Vulgaria*)
2 bunches of young nettle leaves (*Urtica dioica*)
Some chives
1 cup of barley flour
1 tsp salt

Chop the herbs finely and mix in the barley flour and salt. Add enough water to bind it together and place in the centre of the linen or muslin cloth. Tie the cloth securely and add to the pot of simmering venison or wild boar (a pork joint will do just as well). Leave in the pot until the meat is cooked and serve as chunks of bread.

Nettle pudding no. 2

1 bunch of sorrel
1 bunch of dandelion leaves
1 bunch of nettles
4 sprigs of mint (*Menta*) or wild marjoram (*Origanum vulgare*)
1 tsp salt
1 cup fine oatmeal
Water to bind (or if it is springtime, a hunter could have been lucky enough to find some wild birds eggs)

Repeat the process as for recipe No 1 and cook in the pot.

Myrtle pudding

At the Iron Age settlement at Glastonbury in England, the bones of black and red grouse and partridge were found. Of course, edible herbs are not easy to find on the top of moorland so the next recipe is a possible moorland pudding. On the moors in the west of England, there are many small stunted hawthorn trees (*Crataegus monogyna*), so I have added these to the recipe.

2 bunches of hawthorn leaves
1 bunch of sorrel
1 handful of gorse flowers (*Ulex europaeus*)
1 small sprig of myrtle (*Myrica gale*)
1 cup of oatmeal
1 tsp salt

Make as before, and add to the pot with your grouse or partridge. Even though this meat is best left to hang for a few days, it still tastes pretty good when stewed in a pot with this pudding.

Seaweed pudding

>A few leaves of sea lettuce (*Ulva lactuca*)
>1 handful of sea beet (*Beta vulgaris*) this plant grows on the edge of the beach, and tastes like a good spinach
>1 cup of oatmeal
>1 bowl of limpets (*Patella vulgata*) or mussels (*Mollusc*)
>1 egg

Finely chop the sea lettuce and sea beet, add the oatmeal and bind with an egg or water. Cook in the usual way, but add a bowl of limpets or mussels to the pot and use seawater to cook it in. As well as this, some fillets of fish could be added to make a hearty seafood stew with a herb pudding.

10 Clay-baked food

There is some archaeological evidence for the practice of clay-baking foods: biscuit-fired clay fragments have been found in prehistoric cooking pits. These pieces of clay are not fragments of pottery but very friable rough chunks. At a Bronze Age settlement in Cornwall large quantities of burnt clay was found in a hearth. Much of the clay was hard-baked and shapeless but some fragments had signs of smoothing by hand on them and those pieced together formed a sort of shallow dish.

During my research into the possible methods of clay-baking foods I have found that when a joint of meat is wrapped in river clay it is very difficult to carry to the fire to dry before baking. If, however, a piece of wood is placed underneath it, it makes the task much simpler. This wooden plank enables one to move and turn the clay-covered joint around the fire before baking. When the clay is dry the joint is dropped onto the fire and the wooden plank burns away during the cooking process. The clay has to be broken apart at the end of the allotted cooking time (usually two hours for a 3kg joint), but it is always soft and friable since river clay was used. This clay is freely available in most streams in northern Europe; it is not plastic enough to be used for pottery but is wholly adequate when it is used to clay bake food.

This technique has been superseded by cooking 'en-croute' — wrapping meat in a flour and water dough — instead of wet river bank clay. The clay-baking of food is not only a fascinating and novel way to re-enact the cooking techniques of our ancestors, but it is a delicious way to cook meat and fish, sealing all the flavour of the meat within the clay casing. The easiest way to do this is to dig a shallow pit in the open. Buy some raku clay, a clay that has had a lot of sand added to it so that it can stand the thermal shock of being placed in an open fire. Do not use ordinary ceramic clay that has no sand added as it will explode when heated. A good supply of firewood is needed, preferably gorse wood if you can get it. This is by far the best wood for cooking, as it produces a very hot fire and does not spit. This wood is found in a large number of cooking pits on archaeological sites. Therefore, if you have a shallow pit, some raku clay and a large pile of wood, you are ready to clay bake some meat or fish.

Clay-baked food

39 The duck stuffed with blackberries and baked in clay

Clay-baked duck with blackberries (39)

Stuff a medium-sized duck with blackberries and season with salt. Wrap the duck in straw or dried grasses and tie securely with string. Cover the duck with an even layer of clay. This can be done by rolling the clay like pastry or just smearing it over in small pieces. The important thing is to seal the duck completely, leaving no cracks for moisture to escape. This done, place the duck onto a piece of wood and stand it by the fire to dry. Keep turning it every so often so that it dries evenly. When the top and sides are dry, roll the duck gently off the piece of wood and dry the underneath. Now carefully drop the duck into the side of the fire pit, keeping a good fire going. After an hour, turn the duck so the clay fires evenly around the bird. After two hours, the duck should be ready. Using two forked sticks, lift the duck out of the pit and place on a wooden board. Crack open the clay casing and reveal (hopefully) a perfectly cooked duck with a blackberry sauce. As you can imagine, this is not an exact science — the thickness of the clay, the size of the duck and the heat of the fire all play an important part in the overall formula. Yet it is well worth trying as the results can be absolutely delicious.

Clay-baked lamb with mint

Season a loin of lamb with salt and cover the exposed meat with as many mint leaves as possible. Wrap with straw or grasses and tie tightly with string. Cover with clay and bake in a fire pit as above.

Clay-baked pork with myrtle

Season a loin of pork with salt and cover with myrtle leaves. Wrap in straw or grasses as before and cover with clay. Cook as above.

Fish baked in clay

Any whole fish can be used; leave the head on and gut them. Sprinkle with celery seed (*Apium graveolens*) if possible and salt. Wrap in grasses as before and cover with clay. Clay can be smeared directly onto the fish if it is a thick-skinned, scaly fish. If the clay is put directly onto a thin-skinned fish like herring, it tends to make the flesh gritty with the clay when cooked. (**40, 41, 42 & 43**)

Clay-baked trout with ramsons

Cook as before, but after gutting the trout, stuff it with chopped ramson bulbs (or leeks), butter and a little salt. Tie tightly at least two layers of ramson leaves around the fish, then cover in a flour and water paste. Tie to this a good layer of dried grasses and finally the clay. Cook as before in the fire. Any fish cooked in this way is truly wonderful. The flour dough coating seals the ramson leaves in with the butter and the ramson bulbs. It tastes like a garlic-buttered fish. Look out for the wild ramsons in shady places and woodland. This is a recipe well worth trying and would be a signature recipe for any top chef, if he made it.

King carp stuffed with wild plums (colour plate 17 & 44)

When demonstrating ancient cooking techniques in Poland, each day we were given a fish from the previous evening's catch from the lake to cook in clay. One day we were given a huge fish called a king carp, which must have weighed 7kg. Cooking by a wild plum tree and it being autumn, the wild sweet plums were ripe for the picking. So we stuffed this huge fish with wild plums, wrapped it in

Clay-baked food

40 Stage one of clay baking trout. One trout is to be wrapped in grass and the other in Burdock leaves

41 Stage two: the trout are tightly tied with nettle fibre string

42 Stage three: the clay is being wrapped around the fish

43 Stage four: after 40 minutes in an open fire the fish is cooked and juicy and ready to eat

Clay-baked food

44 The carp ready to eat

enormous burdock leaves, tied it with string and covered it with clay and cooked it by the fire for about three hours. When we broke open the clay, it was cooked to perfection and tasted wonderful. I had not tried king carp before and it tasted just like chicken.

Here is a short list of the fish remains found on prehistoric middens in northern Europe: eel, carp, pike, perch, trout, salmon, plaice, bass, mullet, cod and spurdog. At a recent excavation at Zamostie (Upper Volga, Russia), fish traps were found in the river silts; one of them was full of fish skeletons and is dated to the Mesolithic period (10,000 BC). No doubt something happened to the fisherman and he never retrieved his catch waiting for him by the riverbank. The trap was a conical-shaped basket made of split pine pieces, fixed by bands of tree bark string.

Clay-baked wild birds

The easiest way to cook wild birds is to not pluck them but to smear the wet clay directly onto the feathers. There is no need to tie straw or leaves onto the bird before adding the clay as the feathers themselves act as a form of insulation. If, however, a bird with feathers on is hard to get hold of, then wrap in grasses as before. The only disadvantage to this method, is that you cannot eat the skin of the bird; this comes away with the clay and feathers when it is cooked.

Clay-baked hedgehog

Although no one (I hope) is going to go out and hunt a hedgehog for food anymore, it is interesting to note that the traditional method the Romany people used to cook them is to clay bake them in an open fire. When the clay was broken off, the spines came off with it. It is said to taste rather like pork — hence its name.

11 Salt and the seashore menu

Salt

Salt mines in various parts of Europe, such as Cheshire in England and the famous Hallstatt area of Austria, are known to have been exploited by the Celts since a favourite Celtic food was bacon or ham. Strabo the classical writer said

> . . . their flocks of sheep and herds of swine were so very large that they supply an abundance of salt meat . . . not only to Rome but most parts of Italy.

This is a wonderful quotation, as it conjures up a picture of wagons loaded with bacon and hams trundling down mountain passes until they arrive at the Roman road system and distribute their wares as far as the south of Italy. It is possible that they could also have made salted lamb meat, as there is still a tradition of producing salt lamb in northern Britain and Scandinavia today.

However, there are no salt mines in southern Britain but there *is* archaeological evidence for a chain of salt-producing centres along the coast. These are well-documented, one example being a site on the Lizard peninsular in Cornwall. The process involved the filling of rough ceramic trays with seawater and suspending them over a pit fire to produce salt. As the water boiled away more seawater was added until, at the end of the day, a thick block of salt filled the entire tray. These would be left to go cold then the pottery tray was broken from the salt block, which was then ready either to store for use by the village or traded with inland tribes. Due to coastal erosion, one of the Romano-British roundhouses used for salt production is falling away down onto the beach. With every winter's frost, more of the cliff face falls and, with every tide, hundreds of pieces of these salt-producing trays are washed away.

In parts of southern Europe, salt marshes were established to harvest this precious commodity described by M. Mollat du Jourdin:

> The water's path followed a similar route. A conduit was placed into the breakwaters separating the compartments of the marsh. Gravity caused the water to flow toward a reservoir (a tidal reservoir) where

concentration began, then through little canals towards the salt beds; at the lowest level (the evaporating pans), the salt crystallised.

However, in the north the sun is not hot enough for the evaporating pans or reliable enough to use this method so the fire pit and trays were necessary.

In Cornwall today there is a pilchard-salting works that preserves and presses these fish in the traditional way. Huge vats are filled with the day's pilchard catch — un-cleaned and gutted. Bags of salt are then poured onto them and they are left in the vat for six months. The fish are then packed into small barrels and pressed for a few weeks to complete the preservation process (**colour plate 18**). All of the produce of this small works is sent exclusively to northern Italy in the autumn, to be distributed to the mountain villages in the Veneto region. This salted pilchard is used as a seasoning for stews and savoury food, in much the same way as *garum* was in ancient times. *Garum* was a salty, fishy sauce that the ancient Romans used as a seasoning for savoury foods instead of salt. The remains of a Roman *garum*-producing centre in southern Spain can still be visited and one can see the large sunken clay pots used to ferment the salt fish sauce. Strabo refers to the fish-salting industry near Gibraltar, although this was apparently just one of the commodities produced by these people:

> There are exported from Turdetania large quantities of grain and wine, and also an olive oil, not only in large quantities, but also of best quality. And further wax and honey . . . and they have salt quarries in their country, and not a few streams of salt water; and not unimportant either is the fish-salting industry that is carried on, not only from this country, but also from the rest of the seaboard outside the Pillars.

The process was almost identical to the pilchard works, except the fish were pulverised after salting and flavoured with grape juice before being distributed in amphorae to the Roman Empire.

In the course of my research into prehistoric foods, it has become relatively easy to see ancient traditions that have carried on to the present day. One example is the use of butter in the north and olive oil in the south. None though are quite so remarkable as this last uninterrupted line of trade between what were the ancient Cornish Celts and the ancient Romans.

I have many times boiled away sea water on a beach using just a large pan and a driftwood fire. It is fascinating to see the salt starting to appear as the water evaporates — I can recommend it as an interesting experiment. In one day it is possible to produce at least 1kg of salt with very little effort at all. A note of caution, however: due to the pollution in our seas today, ensure that the beach where you are gathering the water is far away from human habitation and therefore relatively pure.

The seashore menu

The peoples who lived by the seashore not only had a ready supply of iodine-rich salt but their diet was much more varied. Since Neolithic times, they could grow crops on the shoreline and hunt for game in the forests inland. In addition, they could harvest the shoreline vegetation, gather shellfish, and the many types of seaweeds that grow on the beach itself.

Laver (*Porphyra umbilicalis*) grows in the inter-tidal zone and rocky coasts around Britain and is still eaten today in parts of Wales and Ireland. The seaweed is easily recognised and gathered as it has translucent purple fronds and crops up at all levels of the shore on rocks and stones. It can also be obtained from most health food stores. In Britain the traditional use for this plant is either as a sauce for mutton or as a laverbread. I will give you the traditional laverbread recipe for you to try.

Traditional laverbread

First wash the laver in plenty of water and then simmer it in very little water until it is cooked (as you would with spinach), but be careful that it does not burn on to the pan. This puree is what is called laverbread. It can be stored in a jar in the refrigerator for a few days and used when required. The favourite way to eat it in Wales is to roll small pieces of this puree in oatmeal and fry it in bacon fat until crisp on the outside. It is then served with bacon for a supper or breakfast meal.

Sea lettuce and curd cheese fritters (45)

Sea lettuce (*Ulva lactuca*) is quite common on British shores. It is found in rock pools attached to stones, is bright green in colour and really does look like lettuce. This recipe is packed full of protein and iodine, and uses some of the simple soft cheese from the *Dairy* chapter.

> 1 good bowlful of sea lettuce
> 1 cup of soft cheese
> 1 egg cup of wholemeal breadcrumbs
> Salt to taste
> 1 cup oatmeal
> Bacon fat or butter for frying

Wash the sea lettuce well and simmer in water until tender (about 30 minutes),

45 A plate of sea lettuce and curd cheese fritters

then chop finely. Drain and add the soft cheese, egg, breadcrumbs and salt. Roll small pieces of the mixture into the oatmeal and fry in the bacon fat or butter. These fritters can be eaten hot or cold.

Carragheen

This seaweed is mentioned in the *Sweets and Puddings* chapter because of its setting qualities. It has no flavour of its own but when simmered with sweet or savoury liquids it will dissolve and set the liquid to a firm jelly. This could have been used to thicken savoury fish stews by just adding a few pieces of the seaweed before serving. It is quite common to find it in rock pools on the west coast of Britain, France and Ireland, but can be bought at health food stores as Irish Moss (**46**).

Shellfish

Prehistoric middens (rubbish dumps) near the sea contain large quantities of shells as a matter of course, usually mussels (*Mytillus edulis*), scallop or clam (*Pecten maximus*), limpet (*Patella vulgata*), cockle (*Cardium edule*) and winkle (*Littorina*

46 A picture of the common Carrageen that I am sure we have all seen on the rocks on holidays without realising what a wonderful jelly-setting, stew-thickening plant it is

littorea). Here is a recipe for winkle butter which tastes remarkably like anchovy paste. It is possible that fish pastes such as these could have been traded with inland tribes for game.

Winkle butter

> Collect a good bucket of edible winkles (A note of caution: be careful that where you gather your shellfish is not on a polluted beach. Pick a beach that is far away from habitation and it should be all right, otherwise buy your winkles) (**colour plate 19**)
> 250g butter
> 28g salt

After collecting the winkles, wash them in fresh water and soak in clean water overnight. Drain and plunge into boiling water, simmer for 15 minutes and drain. Now here comes the labour-intensive part (I find children love this job): with a large safety pin, point bent backward, proceed to pick the winkles out of their shells. Pull off the tough muscle and you should be left with brown coils from the inner shell. These taste delicious if you are fond of shellfish. Mash the winkles with the butter and salt. When you have a smooth paste it is ready to use. It is very good on toast or with bread hot from the oven.

Mussels and bacon

This is a very simple way to eat mussels but very tasty. Fry some bacon in a pan then remove when crisp, put the mussels in the fat and shake over the fire until they have opened. Eat at once with the bacon.

Mussels in horseradish sauce

Cook the mussels in a pan until they open then add some butter, a handful of mustard seeds and some grated horseradish. Cover these with single cream and serve at once.

Oysters and bacon kebabs

Peel a willow stick and trim one end into a spike (or use a skewer). Alternately skewer some oysters with bacon pieces and sea beet leaves, or any other combination, perhaps wild mushrooms, bacon and mussels. Roast them over a fire until cooked. All these recipes make a wonderful beach barbecue, gathering ingredients from the rocks and pools.

Ash-cooked shellfish

Make a herb butter with chervil and a little salt. Arrange any shellfish you have into the hot ash at the edge of your beach fire. As the shells open, add a small piece of the herb butter and eat at once with bread.

Mussel stew with dumplings

>   60 mussels
>   2 cups of milk
>   Salt

1 cup of water
A handful of fine oatmeal

Wash the mussels and put into a large pan with the water, cover and heat until they open. Strain the liquor into a basin and shell the mussels. Lightly toast the oatmeal in a pan and put to one side. Then heat the milk with the mussel juice and add a little salt to taste. Add the mussels but do not let them boil. Put the oatmeal in a large bowl, add one cup of the stock stirring quickly so that it forms knots like small dumplings. Add the oatmeal dumplings and the mussels and eat with lots of bread.

12 Peas, beans and lentils

The first archaeological finds of beans are from 9000 BC in a house near Galilee called Yiftahel; inside the house was a silo of horsebeans which are very much like the Celtic bean. It must have been a favourite crop as they had adapted part of their home to storing it in and making it always available to cook.

However, the evidence for peas being found in northern Europe is sparse although undeniably present. Peas have been found in a Stone Age cave in Hungary, in the mud of a Bronze Age lake dwelling in Switzerland, and in various Bronze Age sites in Britain. This highly sustaining food, packed full of proteins and easily dried for storage, would have been an important part of any prehistoric diet. Peas are not just a good food crop they are also beneficial to the land when rotating crops. All members of the pea family have nitrogen-fixing nodules on their roots so, after a crop of peas a crop of nitrogen-hungry cereals can be grown. Therefore, one type of crop feeds not just the farmers, but also provides the nutrients for the next crop too. Peas can be eaten fresh when they are sweet and young, or allowed to grow and be harvested for storing. They could also have been used as a sugar substitute when fresh. A bowl of early blackberries mixed with bright peas makes a colourful dish, they also taste good together too (**colour plate** 27). Prehistoric societies would not have been hampered — as we so often are — by conventions in food. A pea, if sweet, would have been looked on as a fruit just as much as blackberries. Peas are also very useful for thickening stews and soups or can be ground into flour to add more protein to breads.

Peas

Dried peas with mint and cream

  225g whole dried peas
  25g butter
  1 large bunch of chives
  2 sprigs of mint
  $\frac{1}{2}$ cup of cream
  Salt to taste

Soak the peas overnight in cold water. Drain and cover with water and simmer until they are soft. Drain the peas then put in a dish by the fire to keep warm. Melt the butter in a pan and fry the chopped chives for a minute. Add this to the cooked peas with the chopped mint and cream. Season to taste. Although quite simple, this is a delicious accompaniment to roast meat.

Leftovers recipe

If any of the above pea mixture is left over, it can be made into a nutritious fritter. Add an egg to the peas and enough flour to bind it. Shape into small cakes and roll into a mixture of finely chopped hazelnuts and flour. Brown these cakes on a hot griddle. These pea and nut fritters can be eaten hot or cold and are very good taken on long walks for a savoury snack.

Pease pudding

This is a very traditional way to cook dried peas and can be well suited to cooking in a water pit. Soak peas in water overnight and drain. Cook in fresh water with a few sprigs of thyme. Fry some sorrel and chives or any combination of wild vegetables in some butter until soft. Mix with the cooked pea mixture and add an egg to bind, put the mixture in a cloth that has been greased with butter and floured. Tie the cloth together tightly and drop into a water pit with the cooking meat. It will then absorb some of the meat stock from the pit-cooking process. Alternatively, it can be steamed: Try putting a simple wicker tray over a pot or cauldron of water. Put the pudding on top of this, place a large ceramic bowl over the pudding and set over a fire. This is a very simple and effective steamer which could also be used to cook fish.

Peas and apple

Follow the recipe above but instead of sorrel and chives fried in butter, use chives and chopped crab apples or cooking apples. This is an unusual combination but I think very tasty.

Celtic beans

These are like the modern broad bean (*Vicia faba*) but smaller and with a much thicker outer skin. In Britain these beans are called the 'tic bean' or 'British field bean' and, due to the thick skin, are now mainly cultivated for animal feed. This type of bean has been found throughout Iron Age Europe from Biskupin in Poland to Britain — hence the name 'Celtic Bean'. This bean needs overnight soaking and then boiling in fresh unsalted water for at least three hours. It then has to be processed to destroy the thick outer skin. I find the best way to do this is to grind them between two stones, as one might grind grain. Use a food processor if you do not have the time or inclination to be totally authentic.

Beans and caraway

This is my favourite way to eat Celtic beans.

> 1kg of cooked processed beans
> 25g butter
> 1 big bunch of sorrel
> 1 big bunch of chives
> 1 ramson bulb or two cloves of garlic
> 1 dessert spoon of caraway seeds

Fry the chopped sorrel, chives and ramson in the butter until soft. Add the caraway seeds and the processed beans and salt. Mix well and add a cup of water. Cook gently over the fire until the water is absorbed.

Bean and bacon stew

> 250g fat bacon
> 2 sticks of celery
> A bowl of pignuts (or use chopped parsnips)
> 2 leeks
> 250g mushrooms
> 2 spoons of mustard seeds
> A sprig of thyme
> 500g processed beans

Fry the chopped bacon until crisp and the fat comes out. Chop and fry the celery, leeks, pignuts or parsnip until soft. Add the chopped mushrooms, mustard seeds and thyme and stir well. Add the processed beans, two cups of water and a spoonful of salt. Cook slowly for one hour until all the flavours have combined. Serve with chunks of rye bread and butter.

Savoury bean fritters

>125g butter
>1 bunch of sorrel
>½ cup of chopped hazelnuts
>1 bunch of sea beet or fat hen
>1 handful of grated horseradish
>500g processed beans
>1 egg
>Salt to taste
>Flour to mix

Fry the sorrel in butter with the hazelnuts and sea beet, then add the grated horseradish and the beans. Add the egg and salt and enough flour to make a stiff mixture. Shape into rissoles and fry in more butter until brown. These are good hot or cold.

Sweet bean cakes

I am also adding this recipe to the *Sweet and Puddings* chapter so that you do not miss it. It is really good.

>250g butter
>500g whole wheat flour
>500g processed beans
>500g honey
>1 cup of chopped hazelnuts

Rub the butter into the flour and add the beans. Stir in the honey and hazelnuts. Cook spoonfuls of the mixture on a hot griddle until light brown on both sides. This could be made at any time of the year because all the ingredients are easily stored. These cakes are very nutritious and would have been a good snack, when travelling to another settlement to trade.

Lentils

There is archaeological evidence for lentils at the Iron Age settlements at Biskupin in Poland and in Switzerland. Today, Russia is one of the largest producers of lentils.

Lentils and fat hen or sea beet

    125g lentils
    2 leeks
    1 good bunch of fat hen leaves or sea beet leaves
    25g butter
    1 teaspoon of mustard seeds
    1 litre water
    3 tbs wine vinegar
    Salt to taste

Wash the lentils and soak them for a few hours and drain. Chop the leeks and fat hen and fry it in the butter with the mustard seeds. Add the lentils and water and simmer until cooked. Season to taste and stir in the vinegar.

Lentil and mushroom soup

    125g lentils
    3 whole ramson plants or 2 cloves of garlic and a leek
    25g butter
    1 bowl of chopped mushrooms
    850ml water
    Salt to taste
    1 tsp poppy seeds

Soak and drain the lentils as before. Chop the ramsons and fry in the butter. Add the mushrooms and fry for another few minutes. Then add the water and the lentils and simmer for one hour. Season with salt and add the poppy seeds. Serve with large pieces of wholemeal bread.

13 Herbs and spices

The herbs and spices available to the peoples of prehistoric Europe are, as you can imagine, very different to the ones used today. The trade in spices from the Middle East, and in resinous herbs from the Mediterranean, has always been lucrative. Spices and dried herbs are very potent so they could be transported in small amounts for good profits. We could add some of these condiments to the recipes in this book, but I feel that if we did we would lose the point of the book. This is a book of recipes that could have been made by our northern-European ancestors solely from the bounty that nature has provided for them in their own environment. I will list the herbs and spices that were available with a few serving suggestions for each. Once you begin prehistoric cooking you will no doubt find many other uses for these plants.

Blackcurrant leaves (*Ribes Nigrum*)

Although we all know the fruit of the blackcurrant bush, it is little known that the leaves can also be used as an herb. The leaves taste just like the fruit, only slightly bitter. It can be added to all savoury stew recipes and is still known to be used in Britain in Easter Ledge Pudding (there is a recipe for this in the *Vegetables* chapter), it is basically a mixture of herbs and blackcurrant leaves, which are boiled in a cloth or fried in bacon fat at Easter-time.

Caraway (*Carum carvi*)

This is a member of the carrot family of plants and still widely used throughout Europe — in Germany with cabbage and in Scandinavia in rye bread. These traditional recipes have probably come directly from prehistoric settlements in Europe since rye grain and the wild cabbage plant were available to them. The root of the caraway plant has a culinary history too; it is said that Julius Caesar's army were fed on a bread made of the root processed into flour. Its popularity as a potent herb was probably sustained because of its medicinal properties in aiding digestion. The seeds can be used in almost all savoury and sweet recipes. It is particularly good to bring out the flavour of the Celtic bean, as you will see if you try my bean recipes.

Chervil (*Anthriscus sylvestris*) (cultivated form: *Anthriscus cerefolium*)

I have given the wild Latin name and the cultivated name of this most useful herb for a very important reason. In the wild there are a number of plants that can easily be confused with it that contain deadly poisons. These are particularly Fools Parsley (*Aethusa cynapium*) and Hemlock (*Conium maculatum*). Because of this, I suggest that the cultivated form (*Anthriscus cerefolium*) is either grown from seed or bought from the supermarket. I feel this herb must be included in this book, not only because of its wonderful flavour — a cross between fennel and parsley, but because of its known use in prehistory. At the Skrydstup Barrow in Denmark the remains of a young girl, aged approximately 18 years, were found dating from approximately 1400 BC. This quotation is from a paper produced to commemorate an exhibition of Danish Art Treasures in London in 1948 and is written by H.C. Broholm and M. Hald.

> When the entirely decomposed bottom of the coffin was investigated remains of some plants were found and these indicate the time of year at which the burial took place. Under the cow hide was found a layer of plants consisting of various kinds of grass and parts of umbelliferous flower (wild chervil). As the leaves were neatly preserved and not crumpled, they must have been newly picked when placed in the coffin and since there were neither seeds nor flowers it may be concluded that this fair-haired young girl died in early summer.

Perhaps chervil was her favourite herb or maybe it was picked for her because of the pleasant anise perfume that it gave off; we will never know. Like many others, this herb dries well, keeping not only its green colour but also its aroma. It is a very versatile herb for use in salads and stews and is particularly good with beans and peas. It would have been useful to add some variety to the staple dried legume meals of the winter. Chervil can also be crushed and mixed with butter to baste roasting meats.

Chives (*Allium Schoenoprasum*)

It is still possible to find wild chives growing in most parts of Europe although it has hardly changed in its cultivated form. It is therefore possible to use bought or home-grown chives in recipes and not lose the 'prehistoric' taste. They are wonderful chopped into soft cheeses and the flowers can be added to wild salads to add colour and flavour. Chives can also be sprinkled on eggs or on any savoury food. This herb dries very well and keeps its flavour. I am sure that it would have been kept as an herb throughout the winter to liven up any bland food. In fact, it is one of the few herbs which has a history of continuous use from ancient times.

Herb bennet (*Geum urbanum*)

It is mainly the root of this herb that is used. It has a clove-like flavour and was a favourite pot herb in sixteenth-century Britain. It can be used as one would use cloves in all savoury and sweet recipes.

Horehound (white) (*Marrubium vulgare*)

Native to many parts of Europe, this was a name once cried in the streets of London. This herb was made into cough-drops and also sold in sticks called 'long-life candy', as it was thought to cure all. It is also still used to flavour home-made fudge and could be added to prehistoric sweet cakes. It is very strong so use it in small quantities. Horehound also makes an interesting flavouring for savoury stews.

Horseradish (*Armoracia rusticana*)

The popularity of horseradish as an accompaniment for roast beef and as a flavouring for Danish open sandwiches shows us that if people like the taste of a particular food then there is no need to supersede it with a modern alternative. The root is used and, after peeling, is grated to add hot spice to savoury dishes.

Juniper (*Juniperus communus*)

These are the fruit of a small, evergreen tree native to Europe and Arctic regions. Juniper has a curious life story lasting nearly two full years. It begins as a small berry-like cone, green in colour and only turns black in the second year, which is when the cones are picked. At this stage they are rich in oil, which is the source of their value as a flavouring. A few years ago I happened to be walking in a forest on the Polish- Russian border and saw the wild juniper and pine forests. The grey-leaved bushes, evenly spaced on the clear forest floor between the pines, were really unusual. We were looking out for elk and bison which still roam this area and graze beneath the juniper bushes, giving the whole forest an air of being part of a landscaped parkland. The sweet, sharp flavour of juniper berries gives a delightful smell and flavour to food. They are also used, as is the caraway seed, as an aid to digestion and are cooked in Germany with cabbage. However, the berries are best used with venison, duck, grouse and hare — in fact all rich game meats — flavouring them wonderfully yet also helping to make the meats digestible. This easily dried and stored fruit would have been an invaluable ingredient in most rich prehistoric stew recipes.

Meadowsweet (*Spiraea ulmaria*)

A member of the rose family, this plant grows in meadows and on stream banks. It is a favourite ingredient for adding to herb beers and wines and, in the past, the root was ground and used as a substitute for flour. It can also be roasted as a vegetable, infused with water and drunk as a tea.

Mint (*Mentha*)

There are many varieties of wild mints from Europe and all of them are a useful addition to any gathered wild food, as mint is also well known to aid digestion. Therefore, its addition to savoury foods would have been widespread throughout time. Mint is traditionally used with lamb meals but need not be restricted to this. Finely chopped mint added to a bowl of wild salad with a little salt makes some of the more bitter herbs palatable. If a mint leaf or two are chewed raw, it freshens the mouth and alleviates hunger. I am sure this would not have gone unnoticed with prehistoric children. A few mint leaves infused in boiling water, then sweetened with honey makes a very pleasant drink. Being so abundant and easily dried, I am sure this herb would have been a typical sight hanging in the doorways of prehistoric dwellings.

Mustard (*Brassica rapa*)

How fortunate it is, that the herbs we like to eat with rich meats also have the abilities to help us digest them — mustard is also an aid to digestion. Widespread throughout Europe, it is well evidenced that mustard was used in prehistory. At a

Bronze Age settlement in Cornwall, archaeologists have found a pit in a house with a considerable quantity of mustard seeds in it. There is a possibility that some form of oil was produced from them and it is interesting to note that there are no poisonous plants in this *cruciferae* family. The tender young leaves of the mustard plant are used in salads today. It would have been most valuable to have added the spice to meats and stews, and possibly to flavour sausages which would have been made to preserve meat for the winter.

Bog myrtle (*Myrica gale*)

Myrtle still grows in the marshlands of Europe and is the northern European peoples' most useful and resinous herb. It was found in a Bronze Age barrow at Egtved in Denmark where a residue of myrtle, emmer wheat, cranberries and honey was found in a birch bark container deposited with the body. In Denmark the ingredients of this container have been analysed, and a type of beer produced which is sold to tourists in the area of the barrow. Also, in AD 50, a rich Danish woman from the Iron Age period was buried on the Island of Lolland with a bronze pail containing residues of cranberries, barley and myrtle — perhaps, in life, it was her favourite beer. It is also well known to have been a vital part of ancient beer recipes in Britain. I have found its culinary uses almost limitless, as it seems to change its flavour depending on the food it is cooked with. If cooked with pork, it tastes like sage yet, if cooked with a bowl of blackberries, it tastes like cinnamon. It is also a wonderful accompaniment to fish recipes as it is still used in the Highlands of Scotland. Here is a good recipe so that you can enjoy its flavour; I have made it many times and it is always very popular.

Oat and myrtle cakes

    3 medium sized leeks or ramsons
    125g lard
    1 good sprig of myrtle
    1 tsp salt
    1 cup of medium oatmeal
    1 cup of water

Fry the chopped leeks in the lard until soft. Add the chopped myrtle leaves, salt and oatmeal. Cook, stirring all the time for one minute. Add the cup of water and cook until all of the water is absorbed by the oats. Leave it to go cold, then shape into small cakes and brown on both sides on a hot stone or griddle.

Parsley piert (*Aphanes arvensis*)

Parsley piert is a wild plant unrelated to garden parsley. It was used as a medicinal herb for a variety of ills but does make a good pickle for adding to stews.

Poppy (*Papaver somnifernum*)

The poppy seed is a good natural source of minerals as well as a useful medicinal herb — it can be utilised as an anaesthetic. The seeds are very palatable if used with savouries, sweet foods and breads. They also make a good addition to savoury dumplings that can be added to a rich meat stew. There is a traditional recipe in Europe that could easily have originated in prehistoric times as it is most unusual. Large quantities of poppy seeds are ground to make a sweet cake. There is a recipe for this type of cake in the *Sweets and Puddings* chapter of this book.

Sand leek (*Allium scorodoprasum*)

This is a close relative of garlic and can still be found in the wild on rough grassland. The leaves and bulb are used and provide a mild garlic flavour. We are so used to cooking today with onions and garlic that it is difficult to imagine a kitchen that does not use them. This alternative plant to the onion is quite difficult to find in the wild, so use cultivated leeks as a substitute if required.

Summer savoury (*Satureia Hortensis*) and winter savoury (*Satureia Montana*)

These two savouries are native to Europe. The summer variety is a hardy annual whereas the winter savoury is a shrubby perennial. In Europe it is known to be an antidote for bee stings if a leaf is rubbed on the skin. As the prehistoric peoples also kept bees, perhaps they used it medicinally too. It is also called the 'bean herb' for its wonderful affinity to all bean recipes. It is a member of the mint family and has a peppery flavour, not unlike thyme.

Sweet cicely (*Myrrus oderata*)

Another note of caution if gathering this herb in the wild: it is not unlike hemlock and fool's parsley, so I suggest you try to acquire a plant from a garden centre, or grow your own from seed. Sweet cicely is truly sweet, not just in smell but also in taste, which is like aniseed. It has the ability to sweeten dishes so much that only half the amount of sugar or honey need be used. This would be a great advantage to prehistoric cooks, as honey, although available, would have been precious. Therefore, an herb that could help to sweeten sour fruit would be most useful. The boiled roots can be candied like angelica and used as a sweet. There is a tradition in France of flavouring brandy with it too.

Tansy (*Chrysanthemum vulgare*)

This hardy perennial plant is widely distributed throughout Europe. It was a very popular herb in mediaeval times, eaten particularly in the spring in puddings and with eggs. It is a very bitter herb and has some toxins in it so it must be eaten in small quantities. It is, however, a powerful wormer and maybe prehistoric people used it in the spring — as medieval people are known to have done — to clear out any worm infestation they might have acquired during the winter. As I said, it is very bitter so it is interesting to try with honey and eggs in a light pudding and then try to imagine why — except for the medicinal purposes — it was so popular.

Thyme (*Thymus drucei*)

Thyme is still popular today in most savoury cooking. The wild variety of it is native to Europe but is somewhat milder than the cultivated variety. The thyme flowers, like those of the chive, are a colourful and flavoursome addition to a wild salad. The word 'thyme' comes from the Greek word meaning 'to fumigate' and a type of incense was made from it to drive away insects. Dried thyme also keeps its aromatic qualities for some years, so it would have been very useful to ancient peoples throughout the winter months. It goes very well with sausages and all meat dishes. A pleasant tea can be made from the herb by adding boiling water and sweetening with honey.

Wall pepper (*Sedum acre*)

A now common rock plant in some parts of Europe, this small succulent plant was eaten as a pepper-substitute in savoury dishes.

14 Vegetables

The endless variety of wild edible vegetation available to the northern European peoples could fill a book in its own right so I will only list the vegetation that I have experience with cooking. When one talks about gathering wild vegetation from the hedgerows, most people imagine that one will be poisoned with the first mouthful, yet there are not as many poisonous wild plants as you might expect. Most of these are in the umbellifer family and whenever there is a poisonous plant which is similar to the vegetable proposed in the recipe, I will tell you. I will suggest various recipes for you to try and hopefully you will be inspired to create some new alternatives of your own. The list of wild vegetables is not in alphabetical order, but in the order of the ones I like best. I begin with one of the most common plants and yet one of the richest sources of vitamins and minerals, containing calcium, chlorine, iron, potassium, silicon, sodium and sulphur.

Nettle (*Urtica dioica*)

One of the major uses of the nettle in prehistory was not for eating, but for making nettle fibre thread to be woven into fine cloth. From evidence found in the Neolithic settlements of Switzerland it is known that nettles were made into cloth before linen and wool. Fishing nets have been found made of spun nettle fibre that are so strong they would cut your skin if you tried to break them with your hands. The process to obtain this fibre is to strip the stem bark off the nettle in summer and then boil this in a solution containing wood ashes to remove the green parts. The fibres are then rubbed in dry clay to release the white fibre from the green filaments. What is left is nettle fibre which is pure white and can be spun into thread with a spindle whorl. In Neolithic times a soft nettle cloth would have been very important. Also the need to make a line for fishing strong enough to catch a large fish would have been essential. In early summer, therefore, there would be a lot of nettle gathering going on throughout Europe. As the stems are stripped of their leaves to be processed into thread, there would probably have been a lot of meals including nettles eaten at this time. This food would not be wasted as they had already gathered it for this other important activity. Nettle leaves could also have been dried and saved for medicinal purposes. If some nettle leaves are boiled in water for a few minutes, the liquid is a wonderful antiseptic for healing wounds. I have tried this remedy on a number of occasions and found that cuts bathed in nettle juice heal much quicker and leave no scar. There are also a number of nettle pudding recipes in the *Water Pit* chapter of this book.

Creamed nettles

Gather a large bowl of nettle leaves (wearing gloves), and wash them. Put them in a pot by the fire, or a pan on the stove and add a good piece of butter. Simmer over a low heat, stirring occasionally until tender. Strain, then put back into the pot with some salt, more butter and a little cream. Cook for five minutes and serve sprinkled with chives.

Nettle oatcakes

Cook some nettles as above to the stage when you strain them. Put the strained nettles in a bowl, add a few chopped myrtle leaves, a little salt and an egg. Beat the mixture until smooth then add enough oatmeal to bind the mixture to a stiff dough. Leave to stand for one hour and shape into small cakes. Fry in bacon fat or butter until golden on both sides. These cakes can be served hot with bacon or cold with cheese.

Fried nettles

A plate of fried nettles sounds a little strange but tastes very much like fried seaweed. Pick some young nettle leaves, wash and dry them in a cloth. Heat a pan with some butter or bacon fat and add the nettle leaves. Fry until crisp. This can be crushed and added with salt to a wild salad as a flavouring.

Rock samphire (*Crithmum maritimum*) (47)

This is my favourite wild vegetable. I eagerly await the spring when I can go down to the beach and collect it. Samphire grows on the rocks by the shore and is a succulent little plant with yellow umbellifer flowers. In sixteenth-century Britain there was quite an industry picking samphire and transporting it in barrels of brine to markets in London for sale there. It would have been a useful food source in the winter to the prehistoric people who lived near the shorelines of Europe as

Vegetables

47 A typical location for the delicious rock samphire, found on rocks and walls all around the British coast

it will keep fresh in strong salt brine for a year. It is then soaked in vinegar for a day before use.

Fried rock samphire

The simplest and nicest way to eat it is to boil it in water until soft. Drain and fry in butter until crisp. This is a wonderfully interesting and tasty food to serve to friends at a barbecue. It can also be served just boiled with melted butter.

Samphire pickle

Put the fresh leaves in a brine and leave for two days. Drain and put in a pot with some wild thyme and cover with vinegar (use red wine vinegar). Put the pot in a slow oven or by a campfire and bring slowly to the boil. When cold, store in pots until used. This is a recipe still used in the west of England where this wonderful pickle is served with fish recipes.

Beer samphire pickle

This is also a traditional recipe, possibly coming to us from prehistoric times when home-made beer would have been plentiful. Wash the samphire very well in sour beer, then put it into a large cauldron or pot. Add a little myrtle and dissolve some salt in some more sour beer. Fill the pot with it, covering the samphire, and set it to boil by a fire until the leaves turn bright green. Drain and put into jars, cover with vinegar mixed with a little honey.

Sow-thistle (*Sonchus asper*)

This herb is very rich in minerals and vitamin C, and was mentioned by Pliny. He said that Theseus dined off a dish of sow-thistles before tackling the Minotaur at Athena's suggestion. The seeds of the sow-thistle have been found by archaeologists at Iron Age sites in Denmark. The number of these seeds excavated increases at Viking sites and presumably its worth grew with its popularity.

48 Sea beet and cheese fritters. The sea beet is directly behind the plate

Sow-thistle greens

Wash the leaves and put them in a pan without shaking the water off them. Add a piece of butter and cook until tender. Sprinkle with chives before serving. This makes a good addition to a mixed vegetable pot with dandelions and nettles. It is also good with salads if chopped, but a little bitter.

Sea beet (*Beta vularis*)

The charred roots of sea beet have been identified by environmental archaeologists at the Mesolithic settlement of Tybrind Vig in Denmark. This plant is the ancestor of all modern beets such as beetroot, mangold, chard and spinach. The leaves have not changed much in cultivation as the cultivator's attention was focused on the development of the larger root. The cultivated leaves have size and softness but have lost a lot of the flavour. It grows near the sea and can be easily identified by its thick, shiny, dark green leaves.

Sea beet greens

Wash the beet leaves well and put them over the heat in a pot or pan with a lid. When the leaves have gone a dark green colour drain and serve immediately. The flavour is very like spinach and tastes as though it has been cooked in butter.

Sea beet and cheese fritters (48)

This is a way of making a savoury nutritious snack that can be eaten cold on a long walk, or for a journey wrapped in some uncooked beet leaves. Cook two handfuls of beet as above and drain. Chop the cooked beet and place in a bowl with a cup of wholewheat breadcrumbs. Add a cup of chopped hard cheese such as cheddar and a little salt. Bind with two eggs and shape into small cakes. Roll in rye flour and fry in a pan with some butter or bacon fat. These can be eaten hot — the cheese melts in little pockets within the fritters. These are very tasty and one of my children's favourites.

Beet and nut fritters

Follow the recipe for beet and cheese fritters but add a cupful of chopped hazelnuts instead of the cheese. If fried in butter, this makes a good vegetarian fritter for a barbecue.

Fat hen (*Chenopodium album*) (49)

This is one of the most common seeds found on prehistoric sites apart from grain seeds. Its seeds are found in bog bodies in Saxony, Germany, Lindow Man in Britain and Tollund Man in Denmark. It is very nutritious as it contains more calcium and iron than cooked cabbage or spinach, and more calcium and vitamin B1 than raw cabbage.

Fat hen greens

Cook as directed for sea beet and serve with butter for a spinach-like vegetable. It can also be used as a substitute in all the sea beet recipes. Fat hen grows in most northern regions and is easy to find, usually as a weed in a garden.

49 A picture of fat hen when it is in seed; it is a very familiar garden weed but tastes too good to throw onto the compost heap

Sea kale (*Crambe maritime*)

This grand plant grows on the shingle and sand on the edge of the beach. The plant used to be cultivated *in situ* and was tended by coastal dwellers from the spring until the early summer. When the first young shoots appeared in the spring, gravel and sand were piled up against them to blanch the shoots. This was done throughout the spring then the sand pulled back and the shoots harvested. The plant is very tough and bitter if it is not blanched in this way.

Sea kale shoots

Cut the shoots into manageable lengths and boil in salted water for 30 minutes. Serve with butter, like asparagus.

Wild celery (*Apium graveolens*)

This plant grows in damp places and at the edge of reed beds. It is a very strong-smelling plant, it grows up to 1-2ft high with shiny yellow green leaves shaped like the garden variety. In an attempt to blanch out some of the strong flavour, it was brought into cultivation in medieval times in Britain. The leaves can be gathered and dried to add flavour to stews in the winter. The most valuable part of the plant is the seed though which, when crushed with salt, makes a wonderful spicy seasoning for all fish dishes. Warning: do be careful when identifying it. When in doubt, use organic non-blanched varieties.

Chickweed (*Stellaria media*)

This plant has been in Europe since the late glacial period yet, to look at it, one would think it could not stand even a light frost. It is a light green, succulent edible weed and not to be confused with the dark green hairy mouse ear chickweed which is not edible. Any gardener will recognise it instantly as a pest to be removed to the compost heap with all the other garden weeds. It is, however, a plant that in times gone by was sold at market stalls for salads, or for a wholesome tender vegetable. It is one of the few plants which is rich in copper, which is beneficial to a balanced diet. Wash this herb, dry it and add to a wild salad. This is a welcome addition in the early winter months as it is not affected by severe weather.

Chickweed greens

Wash the plant and put it in a pot with a little butter and salt, and simmer until tender. Sprinkle with chives and serve.

Ramsons (*Allium ursinum*) (colour plate 22)

This member of the onion family is a beautiful sight when discovered by chance in the wild, yet one knows of its presence before one sees it because of its strong garlic smell. Another name for it is 'wood garlic', as it is found in damp shady places. The leaves are broad and the flowers a ball of white starry blossom. All parts of the plant can be used, but it is best eaten raw as it loses a lot of its flavour when cooked. Chopped fine in salads is best, or as a garnish to any savoury meal.

Marsh thistle (*Cirsium palustre*)

This is the tall thistle that is found growing in marshland and looking like an elaborate candlestick standing tall among the sedge grasses. Although it looks unappetizing, it is a wonderful vegetable. Handle with care when picking it though, as it has very sharp prickles. Also be careful when walking to cut it as it tends to grow in very swampy conditions. The peeled stems of this plant, eaten raw, are like a juicy celery and very good for a snack, or to be chopped into a salad. I am sure when prehistoric people were walking into the marshes to gather sedge grasses to make hats and baskets, they would have had a snack of marsh thistle on a hot day.

Braised marsh thistle

If you like braised celery, then you will like braised marsh thistle as the taste and texture are almost identical. Pick the plant before the middle of the summer as it starts to become tough. Carefully peel the main stems of the plant and chop into sticks. Wash and put in a pot by the fire with a little butter and some salt. Simmer until tender and serve immediately

Bistort (*Polygonum bistora*)

This plant also inhabits wet ground, mainly on hilly pastures and is native to most parts of Europe. In the north of England, the tradition of making a savoury pudding with this herb is still so strong that each year they have a Dock Pudding-Making Championship. As you can imagine, there are many variations on this dish so I will give you the recipe for the most traditionally made example.

Easter ledge or Bistort pudding

> 1 good bunch each of bistort, nettle and dandelion leaves
> 6 large blackcurrant leaves
> 1 leek or some ramson leaves
> $\frac{1}{2}$ cup of oatmeal
> $\frac{1}{2}$ cup of whole barley
> Water to cover
> 1 tsp salt
> 1 egg
> Bacon fat or butter to fry

Wash, dry and finely chop all the herbs and the leek, and put into a bowl with the oatmeal and barley. Add the salt, cover with water and leave overnight. Put into a greased dish and bake slowly in an oven for 1.5 hours. (In prehistoric times a clay clome oven could have been used for this. See **colour plate 13**.) Just before serving, add a beaten egg and return to the oven for a few more minutes. An alternative method is to add the egg after soaking, slowly fry the whole mixture in bacon fat and serve with bacon.

Burdock (*Arctium minus*) (50)

If you have ever walked through an overgrown meadow in the late summer, you will recognise this plant. It is the one that deposits its round, ball-shaped burrs on any passing person, dog or horse. Its leaves are huge and look very much like a rhubarb. In Britain it is still made into a well-known and popular children's drink with dandelions. In Japan the plant is cultivated for the tough black roots, which are finely chopped and put into savoury dishes. It has a smell and flavour all its own so I will not try to describe it. It is the stems that are mostly used as a vegetable though. If picked in May (no later) the hard outer peel of the stem is stripped off to leave a thin, pencil-like stick. This is very good raw, chopped in salads or boiled and served with butter (like asparagus). The leaves are also very useful for wrapping fish before clay baking.

50 The Burdock plant, which most people recognise at this stage as it releases its burrs onto any passing animal or person

Silverweed (*Potentilla anserine*)

Silverweed is an almost universal plant that is native from Lapland to New Zealand, from China to Chile and grows in most types of soil. The leaves of this plant are easily identified for its silvery, feathery leaves covered with downy white hairs. It is thought to have been a cultivated crop in prehistoric times. It is the roots that were harvested, eaten raw, or boiled, or baked. They were also ground into a flour after baking and made into a bread. In more recent times, it has been used as a famine food as it is so abundant in the wild.

Pignut (*Conopodium majus*)

This slender umbellifer plant flowers in June and has leaves like fennel. It is always found in my part of the world, surrounding prehistoric sites in abundance. I am sure it was cultivated as it is one of the best root crops of the wild harvest. It was a popular wayside snack for children until recent times. The roots cannot be pulled up; one has to use a knife or your finger to follow the slender stem underground to find the root. The root is the size and shape of a shelled hazelnut, and has a thin skin which is easily peeled away to reveal this juicy white ball. It can be eaten raw — a taste not unlike a cross between parsnips and hazelnuts — or it can be boiled or roasted to be added to savoury dishes.

Early purple orchis (*Orchis mascula*)

I am not suggesting that anyone goes out and digs up these now rare and beautiful flowers, but it is interesting to find out why they have in fact become so rare. The tubers of the orchis contain a starchy substance called bassorine, which is said to have more nutritive ingredients in it, than any other single plant. One of these is said to be sufficient to sustain a man for a whole day. It is still widely used in the Middle East, being eaten raw or cooked, although it is mostly made into a drink by drying the tubers in the sun and grinding them into a rough flour. This flour is mixed with honey and stirred into hot milk until it thickens. In Britain a similar drink was made in Victorian times; it was mainly made with water and spirits were added to it later. It was a food for the workers and, in some cases, it was made so thick it had to be eaten with a spoon. The early purple orchis cannot be easily cultivated as it depends on a peculiar association with fungi during its young stages and may take years to reach maturity. So the orchis for this popular life-sustaining food had to be gathered from the wild, hence the rarity of these plants today.

White waterlily (*Nymphaea alba*)

This is the common water lily still found in sheltered ponds and lakes. It is the tubers of this plant that were eaten as a sustaining food in the past. These tubers can grow six feet below the surface of lakes and ponds which were probably infested with leeches. Therefore, the tubers of the water lily, which I have not tried, must be either very sustaining, or a great delicacy to merit the effort in obtaining them.

Salad vegetables

There is an almost infinite range of possible plant combinations for a wild salad, so I will list the ones that I tend to use the most.

Sheep's sorrel (*Rumes Acetosella*)

This very common plant, found in most prehistoric sites, is one of my basic ingredients for most meals. It has a taste of sharp apple skins when eaten raw. This is very good chopped in a salad with any other combination of plants.

Shepherd's purse (*Capsella bursa-pastoris*)

This plant is found on sites from Bronze Age Britain, to Iron Age Denmark. It is a very common plant in most gardens and the bane of the gardener as it grows and seeds itself everywhere. However, it does taste wonderful. The little leaves taste exactly like watercress and are a very good addition to any salad.

Dandelion (*Taraxacum officinale*)

This plant needs no description as it is most common throughout Europe and grows on most people's lawns and in parkland. The roots are most commonly made into a coffee substitute when roasted, and its flowers are still popular for wine-making. The leaves are cultivated in France to add to salads. Although they are very bitter eaten on their own, they are good when mixed with other plants.

Jack-by-the-hedge (*Alliaria petiolata*) (colour plate 25)

Another name for this plant is 'hedge garlic'. It can be seen as early as February in Britain if there has been a mild winter. This delicate plant is wonderful in a wild salad, but not so good if cooked as it loses its delicate garlic flavour completely.

Bedstraw (*Galium sp.*)

This plant is found on many prehistoric sites and is native to Europe. It is an annual herb that climbs up banks and hedgerows. The stem is covered with hook bristles that cling to clothing when brushed past. Chopped finely into salad it is very pleasant.

Yarrow (*Achillea millefolium*)

This plant is most famous as a wound healer and as the ingredient to make a tea to cleanse the blood. It is an interesting addition to a wild salad if used in small quantities as it has a strong resinous taste.

Hawthorn leaves (*Crataegus monogyna*)

The leaves of this small tree are usually the first indication that spring has arrived. These light green leaves provide a wonderful base to a wild salad with a pleasant nutty flavour. Eat hawthorn leaves only in the spring as they become very tough by the summer.

Beech leaves (*Fagus sylvatica*)

The leaves of the beech are soft and translucent in April and make a wonderful salad. They have the flavour of mild cabbage, yet are sweet.

Flowers in salads

There are many flowers that can be added to a wild salad, not only to make a bowlful into a wonderfully colourful sight, but also to add nutrition to the dish. Here is a list of the best (**colour plate 23**):

- Clover (*Trifolium sp.*)
- Chives (*Allium schoenoprasum*)
- Gorse (*Ulex Europaeus*) **(colour plate 24)**
- Primrose (*Primila vulgaris*)
- Violet (*Viola ordorata*)
- Heather (*Calluna vulgaris*)
- Elder (*Sambucus nigra*)

15 Yeast, wines, beer and teas

It is well recorded that the Celts loved wine and beer and this was so for the peoples who preceded them. The fermenting of liquids to produce alcohol must be one of the earliest of man's activities. Simple beer would have been consumed as a regular drink and among its many virtues as a beverage it contained vitamins that are often lacking in a cereal-based diet. In ancient Egypt, barley was used to make beer and it was said that everybody drank it every day. To make it the Egyptians first moistened barley with water and left it to stand. Then they mixed the moist grains with lightly-baked barley loaves in a large jar and added more water. This mixture was left to ferment. When ready, the mixture was very thick and had to be strained before drinking.

The yeast cycle

The acquisition of yeast for prehistoric peoples revolved around a yearly cycle. This was also so for many aspects of their lives, following the seasons and festivals. The yeast cycle for bread-making is totally reliant on wine and beer production as mentioned earlier. The generally accepted festivals of the Bronze Age are linked with the cycles of the sun: the solstices and the equinoxes that divided the year into four three-month seasons. In Celtic days the year was also divided into four, but at different times. If a new wine were set to ferment after each festival, it would be ready in time for the next, three months later. The start of the Celtic New Year also coincides with the ripening of the elderberry (**colour plate 26**) and the making of elderberry wine. This fruit is one of the richest natural sources of wild yeast in northern Europe.

Put a large quantity of elderberries (about 3kg) into a vessel such as an open-ended barrel if you can get one. Add 1.5kg of honey and 4 litres of spring water. Keep it in a warm place and after a few days it will start to ferment. Continue to keep it in a warm place covered with a cloth for two months. Taste it every so often and add more honey if it becomes dry. At the end of two months, strain the wine off the top of the sediment and store until needed. The wine should be stored after it becomes dry again since, at this time, it is in a state of suspended fermentation. It can be sealed without the risk of it beginning to ferment and exploding the containers as gases build up. The classical historian Diodorus Siculus says of the Celtic Iberians of the Pyrenées '... for their food they eat meat in abundance and a drink of wine mixed with honey'.

So the wine was probably stored dry to stop it fermenting again and honey was mixed with it to sweeten it before drinking. However, the sediment that is left in the barrel is a concentrated form of wild yeast. Some of this can be added to another fruit or herb, to make a yeast starter for another wine with the addition of more honey and water. The same yeast concentrate can be added to malted wheat or barley to make different kinds of beers. Therefore, there would automatically be a constant supply of yeast for bread-making — a yeasted bread can be made if some sediment is added to flour and left to rise in the normal way. I have succeeded in drying this sediment in shallow trays in the sun until it looks like a piece of rubber. I have then stored it in a container sealed with beeswax and left it for some months. I then added a little warm water and some honey to a piece of it and kept it in a warm place for a day. The yeast revived and I was able to add it to flour and make a yeasted bread with it.

However, there is another way to acquire wild yeast without making wine. This is by making leaven with barley flour. Mix a small quantity of barley flour with warm water to make a dough. Form it into a round shape and make a dent in the centre about half way through. Put the dough onto a plate and cross it lightly with a knife twice. Fill this dent with warm water and leave it in a warm place for a few days. The dough will have fermented by then and split open like a over-ripe fruit. It can be used to make yeasted bread by adding this dough to flour, using it as a yeast starter. This is very effective but not quite so much fun as making a good wine to acquire the yeast for your bread.

Beer

Old English and European country inns always used to brew their own beers and many farmhouses did likewise. Although hops and malt form the basis for beers and ales today, this was not always the case. Any herb tea could be fermented and turned into an alcoholic drink. Here are a few for you to try, the first being a mild brown ale. It used to be made very weak and almost non-alcoholic and was drunk from breakfast to bedtime by most people before coffee and tea became fashionable. Also, hops have been used in Europe since prehistoric times for brewing ale, although they were not introduced into Britain until the sixteenth century.

51 Mild brown ale in a replica Beaker Pot.

Mild brown ale (51)

>150g hops
>1 cup of wheat malt (sprouted and baked wheat grains)
>32 litres water
>1.5kg honey
>A cup of wild yeast or 60g yeast

Slowly boil the hops and malt together with half the water for 50 minutes. Then strain over the honey and add the rest of the water. Allow it to cool and, when warm, add the yeast. Cover the tub with a cloth and allow to ferment for four days. It is then ready to bottle and drink as required. I suggest you try this recipe in smaller quantities to see if you like it.

Strong ale

>4 litres water
>500g malted barley grains
>500g honey

2 handfuls of hops
½ cup wild yeast or 30g yeast

Heat two litres of water until hot but not boiling and add the malted barley grains and honey. With the rest of the water, boil the hops and simmer for 10 minutes. Strain both the liquids and put in a large tub with the yeast when it is warm. Leave covered with a cloth for three days. This will ferment vigorously and a large container will be needed as it will rise up quite a lot. This is then ready to drink or bottle. Make sure that you put it in strong bottles so that it will not explode.

Meadowsweet ale

A bunch of meadowsweet (*Spiraea ulmaria*)
A bunch of agrimony (*Agrimonia eupatoria*)
A bunch of betony (*Betonica officinalis*)
A bunch of raspberry leaves (*Rubus idaeus*)
A sprig of hyssop (*Hysopus officinalis*)
12 litres water
1.5kg honey

Boil all the herbs together (apart from the hyssop) in the water for 15 minutes. Strain, add the honey and hyssop and mix well. When cool, strain again and bottle.

Spruce beer

A small spruce twig (*Abies nigra*), approximately 30g in weight
30g hops
1 sprig of yarrow leaves (*Achillea millefolium*)
1 bunch of blackcurrant leaves (*Ribes Nigrum*)
2kg honey
20 litres water
2 cups of yeast or 30g dried yeast

Boil the spruce twig in a little water for 30 minutes, strain and put aside. Add all the other ingredients except the yeast to the rest of the water and boil for 30 minutes. Strain when cool and add the yeast. Leave covered for 24 hours then bottle.

Three flowers beer

> 1 handful of hops
> 1 handful of violet flowers (*Viola ordorata*)
> 1 good bowl full of elderflowers (*Sambucus nigra*)
> 11 litres water
> 2kg honey
> 1 cup of white wine vinegar

Boil the hops and violet flowers in water for five minutes and strain. Add the elderflowers, honey and vinegar, cover and leave in a warm place for two days. Strain and bottle. This is a very pleasant drink fermented by the wild yeast on the elderflowers.

Nettle beer

> 1 saucepan-full of nettles
> 30g hops
> 500g malted grain
> 2 litres water
> 250g honey
> ½ cup of wild yeast or 30g yeast

Wash the nettle leaves, add the hops and malted grain and boil with the water for 30 minutes. Strain and add the honey. When warm, add the yeast and leave to ferment for three days. Strain and drink after a week or two when it starts to become alcoholic.

Dandelion (*Taraxacum officinale*) and burdock (*Arctium minus*)

The same recipe as for nettle beer, but use three parts burdock leaves to one part dandelion flowers. A non-alcoholic version of this drink is still made commercially in Britain, as a children's drink.

Wine

The first wine that you make should be elderberry to provide the wild yeast starter for all the rest (see chapter head).

Elderberry wine

>3kg elderberries (no stalks)
>4 litres water
>1.5kg honey

Put the elderberries and honey into a large container with the water and leave in a warm place. Make sure it is well covered with a lid or cloth, as the vinegar fly will ruin it. After a few days the liquid will start to ferment. Stir the liquid and taste it every few weeks for two months when it will be ready. If it is very dry when you taste it, then add another kilogram of honey. After two months you should have a good rich, red wine. Strain and bottle it only when it is dry to taste. If you bottle it when it is sweet, it will start to ferment again and blow up your bottles. As long as it is dry it is in a state of suspended fermentation. It can be sweetened just before drinking with more honey. If you are keen to make wine and it is not the time of year for elderberries, then use commercial dried yeast until you can make it. I recommend this wine is made not just for the yeast but because it tastes so good. There are many old stories in Britain that drinking a glass of elderberry wine a day is very good for you. There has been some recent research on this and it has been found that elderberries actually have anti-carcinogens in them. So maybe there is a grain of truth in this story after all.

English sack

This is an old English recipe from 1736, but I am sure it was made long before.

>A handful of fennel roots (*Foeniculum vulgare*)
>A sprig of rue (*Ruta graveolens*)
>4 litres water
>1.5kg honey

Boil the rue and fennel root in the water for 30 minutes, strain and add the honey. Boil for a further two hours, skimming from time to time, before emptying the liquid into a cask. Allow the sack to ferment for one year before drinking and bottling.

Rosehip wine

>1.5kg rosehips
>4 litres water
>A bunch of sorrel leaves (*Rumex acetosa*)
>2kg honey
>1 cup of wild yeast or 30g yeast

Boil the rosehips in water for ten minutes with the sorrel leaves. Thoroughly mash the rosehips in the water and then strain through muslin. Pour the liquid into a vessel and add the honey and yeast. Leave in a warm place with a cloth over it for at least two months. Then bottle and leave for a year before drinking.

Elderflower champagne

>2 elderflower heads
>500g honey
>3 tbs white wine vinegar
>4 litres cold water

Pick heads that are in full bloom and put them into a bowl with the other ingredients and cold water. Cover and leave for 24 hours, then strain and bottle. Make sure that you bottle this in plastic fizzy drink bottles or champagne bottles as it will ferment and explode an ordinary bottle. This is ready to drink in two weeks as a sparkling soft drink which is wonderful to take on picnics, or you can keep it for a year when it becomes dry and alcoholic.

Birch sap wine

Tapping a birch tree for its sap is quite easy and will not harm the tree, provided you follow these five rules:

>1 Tapping should only be done in the first fortnight of March.
>2 Only mature trees should be used (those of at least a 9in diameter).
>3 Bore only as far as necessary for the tube to stay in place, about 1in. (The sap rises just near the bark, not right at the heart of the trunk).
>4 Do not take more than 4 litres per tree.
>5 Plug the hole with a cork or wooden peg when the tapping is finished. (You can use the same hole next year.)

Push one end of a plastic or rubber tube firmly into the bored hole and direct the other end into a jar on the ground. Cover the top of the jar with some muslin to prevent insects getting in. Leave the jar in this position for two days and you should have 4 litres of sap. This tastes wonderfully refreshing and slightly sweet if drunk straight from the tree.

> 4 litres birch sap (*Betula pendula*)
> ½ cup of white wine vinegar
> 1.5kg honey
> 1 small bowl of dried elderberries (you can dry your own or buy them from wine-making shops)

Add some warm water to the elderberries and leave overnight in a warm place to reconstitute and revive the yeasts on the skin. Add this to the birch sap and the other ingredients and leave covered to ferment. Strain and bottle after six months. Save the sediment for another wine or for bread. This wine needs a year to mature before drinking.

Blackberry *(Rubus fruticosus)* and raspberry *(Rubus idaeus)* wine

This is a truly wonderful wine — rich and fruity and just the thing to drink on a cold winter's evening whilst remembering the summer.

> 1.5kg blackberries
> 1.5kg raspberries
> 8 litres water
> 500g honey
> 1 cup of wild yeast or 30g yeast

Pour very hot water onto the fruit in a large container and mash when warm. Add the honey and yeast (you do not need too much honey as the fruit is very sweet). Cover with a cloth and leave in this container for two months. Taste every so often and add some more honey if it is too dry. Then strain and store in its dry state and sweeten if needed before drinking.

Metheglin with caraway

This is a honey wine that is usually flavoured with herbs but I think this recipe would have been made in prehistoric times as a drink to help digestion. It tastes like Danish akavit but is not as strong.

> 4 litres water
> 3kg honey
> 1 cup of wild yeast or 60g yeast
> 1 handful of caraway seeds

Heat the water until it is hot but not boiling, then stir in the previously warmed honey until dissolved. Cool and add the yeast. Put the vessel in a warm room to ferment. When the fermentation ceases after about one month, strain the clear honey must from the vessel and put into another container. Add the caraway seeds and store in a container with a lid for one year. This mead is said to be best drunk after maturing for two years.

Barley wine

> 500g barley grain
> 1.5kg honey
> 4 litres water
> 1 cup of wild yeast or 30g dried yeast

Put the grain into a large vessel and cover with boiling water, add the honey and stir well. When warm, add a cup of wild yeast or dried yeast and cover with a cloth. Put into a warm place and allow to ferment. After two weeks this liquid is a very potent yeasty drink. Strain most of the liquid off, but leave some still in the vessel. Add to this some more water and a little more honey, and leave for another few weeks and strain again. I am sure this would have been a favourite drink for the Celts, either made with barley or wheat. As with all grain wines, it is very strong and very easy to make, hence I am sure it would have been popular. It is very difficult to judge the strength of these wines as it depends on the honey or sugar in the fruit, or the strength of the yeast. So sample with care.

Teas and soft drinks

Teas can be made by pouring boiling water over any herb and allowing it to infuse. So as long as the herb is pleasant to taste and edible you can make a tea out of anything you like. Some of my favourites are mint, elderflower, and a combination of heather flowers (*Erica cinerea*), wild strawberry leaves (*Fragaria vesca*) and bilberry leaves (*Vaccinium myrtillus*). A pleasant drink can be made, by adding a cup of any type of fruit to boiling water and allowing it to steep until all the flavour is released. Here are a few very old recipes for country peoples' drinks that you might like to try.

Linseed tea

The flax plant that produces linseed is known to have been cultivated from Neolithic times for the linen thread as well as the oil-rich seed. Here is a traditional recipe that could well have come to us from Neolithic times.

> 1 litre cold water
> 1 handful of linseeds
> $\frac{1}{2}$ cup of malted wheat
> $\frac{1}{2}$ cup of honey

Wash the linseeds and put them into a pan with the water and the malted grains. Bring the water to the boil and reduce the heat, simmering for 20 minutes. Add the honey and simmer for another five minutes. Strain and serve. It is also said that this drink is very good for sore throats and colds.

Barley water

> 1 handful barley
> 2 litres water
> $\frac{1}{2}$ cup of honey
> 2-3 crab apples or 1 cooking apple

Scald the barley with boiling water and strain. Then put the scalded barley into a pan with two litres of water and half a cup of honey, and bring to the boil. Chop up a few crab apples or a cooking apple, and add it to the boiling water. Leave it to go cold and strain.

Slackers

> 1 cup of fine oatmeal (as fine as flour)
> 250g honey
> 4 litres water

Slackers was said to be the best drink to slake the thirst and was said to be very strengthening after hard work. Put the oatmeal and honey into a pan and mix together with a little warm water. Then add 4 litres of boiling water and stir well. Leave until cold before drinking.

Blaand (sparkling whey)

This is a most interesting recipe that I found in an old Scottish cookery book. Drinking fermented whey is still popular with some nomadic peoples today in distant parts of Russia. This is called Kumys and thought of as the 'best beverage in the steppes' and is made of fermented mares milk. Milk was also used to make alcoholic drinks such as milk vodka. Some form of fermented whey would have probably been a common recipe wherever large herds of cattle were managed. This Shetland beverage is simply the whey of buttermilk left to ferment in an oak cask and used at the proper stage. To make the whey, pour enough hot water on the buttermilk to make it separate and drain the whey off the curd (which may be pressed and eaten with cream). Pour the whey into a cask and leave it undisturbed until it reaches the fermenting, sparkling stage. It is a delicious and most thirst-quenching drink and sparkles in a glass like champagne. After the sparkle goes off, it becomes flat and vinegary, but may be kept at the perfect stage by the regular addition of fresh whey. Blaand used to be in common use in every Shetland cottage, and was at one time given by fashionable doctors to consumptives under the name of the *Sour Whey Cure*.

16 Sweets and puddings

The major sweetener in prehistoric times was honey yet there is also a large quantity of substances that can be added to food to make it sweet. There are many wild fruits that could have been used as sweeteners such as blackberries, raspberries, cherries, plums, wild strawberries and bilberries — remains of all these have been found in lake villages in prehistoric Switzerland. The reeds that formed the thatch for their dwellings were also a source of sugar. The fresh green stem is cut and left in the spring and a sugary sap forms around the cut. If this is left it can be picked off and eaten as a sweet. The American Indians used to process the reed sugar by picking the green stems in the spring and drying them. When totally dry, the stems were pulverised between stones over fine cloths. The white powder was then strained from the stem debris and mixed with a little

52 Crab apples, blackberries and myrtle leaves, a good and spicy combination for a sweet pudding

water. Small balls of this paste were then cooked by a fire until they doubled in size and were ready to eat. Even though I have always wanted to try this, I have never done so because it would be dangerous to do so where I live in Cornwall. Reeds are known to soak up all kinds of organic compounds and are now used on an industrial scale to soak up pollution and heavy metals in water runoff from derelict Cornish tin mines. Therefore, if you live in a mining area, eating any part of a plant that absorbs heavy metals is not advisable. If you live in a chalk area, it would be safe to try this and see just how sweet the reed sap really is.

Bread made with freshly harvested grain is full of natural sweetness, this fades as the grain is stored throughout the winter months. Young peas make a delicious sweetener to cakes and puddings. Various wild flowers, such as clover flowers, can also be added as a sweetener. I have done some research with clover flowers to see if the sweetness they contain could in some way be preserved. I collected a bowl full of flowers on a dry sunny day and slowly dried them in an oven for an hour. The flowers turn brown and become crisp to the touch, they also taste very much like sweet liquorice. In this dry state, they can be stored and added as a flavouring to various foods — both sweet and savoury. When making sweet recipes and puddings, it is important to understand how special the food that you are making would have been to our prehistoric ancestors. Although honey would have been available all year round (since it has exceptional storing qualities), it would have been a rich or lucky man's food (that is, if a wild hive were found in the forests). It would have had high trading value too, so that the ordinary people would have had to wait for the abundance of wild fruits to satisfy their sweet tooth. There are eggs in some of these recipes, which would have been a very seasonal food as it is very difficult to store them adequately. Any eggs would have been eaten, though probably the most common would have been duck eggs gathered from the marshlands. The community would have gathered the water reeds from the marshes every winter and spring to repair their thatched roofs, or for basketry. I should imagine that duck eggs would have been relished by the reed gatherers on their return to their settlements. In the highlands of Scotland there is still a tradition of climbing the high sea cliffs to acquire seagull's eggs in the springtime. So if you wish your reconstructed prehistoric meal to be truly authentic, then recipes containing eggs should be made only in spring and early summer. The rich spring grasses enriched the milk of the herds of cattle, so many of these recipes include cream. 'Beestings', the name in Britain for the first milk that the cow produces after having a calf, usually only for the first three days, would also have been enjoyed.

Beesting pudding

> 500ml beestings
> 1 pinch of salt
> 5ml honey

Place all of ingredients into a bowl and bake in a slow oven for one hour until solid. Store in a cold place overnight. Serve in small quantities (it is very rich) with a little honey. It tastes like a rich and creamy egg custard.

Junket

This is a less rich, traditional country pudding that I am sure is still well known throughout northern Europe. In our more recent history, before refrigeration and home freezers, people would eat seasonally. When a lot of calves were born to the herd then recipes would be made to use up this plenty. My own experience when first owning a house cow shows how important it is not to waste the gallons of milk each day that she produces. One has to find recipes that include large quantities of milk just to keep up with it. My house cow produced four gallons of milk per day after calving, one gallon of which was thick, yellow cream. This recipe for junket is a good simple way of using the milk up. If you can get milk fresh from the cow, so much the better; if not, fresh whole milk from the dairy is just as good. One litre of milk is put in a large bowl after being just warmed in a pan. Stir 10ml of rennet into this and leave to set. Serve as cold as possible in individual bowls with just a little cream and a spoonful of honey.

Pancakes

An easy, pleasant way to use up large quantities of milk and eggs is to make pancakes.

> 125g wholewheat flour
> 500ml milk
> 1 pinch of salt
> 2 eggs

Mix all of the ingredients together with a whisk until you get a smooth mixture. Leave to stand for two hours, then cook in small spoonfuls on a hot griddle or pan. These pancakes can be served hot with honey and cream, or cold spread with butter and honey.

Hazelnut pancakes

> 125g wholewheat flour
> 500ml milk
> 1 pinch of salt
> 125g honey
> 125g roasted hazelnuts (stored from the previous year)

Mix all of the above together, adding the nuts after the mixture is smooth. Cook in small spoonfuls or place into a large flat tray in the oven. Serve in squares when hot with more honey and cream.

Sweet dumplings

> 500g wholemeal flour
> 2 eggs
> 125g honey
> Milk to mix to a thick batter

Whisk the eggs, honey and flour together. Gradually add the milk. Bring a pan of water to the boil or put a fireproof pot into the side of a campfire. When the water is boiling, drop spoonfuls of the batter into the water. Boil for 10 minutes until cooked and then ladle out and eat immediately while hot. Hazelnuts could be added to this to make a richer dumpling.

Fruit dumplings

> 500g wholewheat flour
> 250g wild fruit any of the types mentioned earlier
> Water to mix to a stiff batter

Cook as above in a pan of boiling water and serve hot with cream. This recipe has no eggs in it, so it could have been made in the autumn and summer when the wild fruits were plentiful.

Black dumplings

> 500g wholemeal flour or oatmeal

250g lard or pig fat
125g honey
500g blackberries and elderberries
Water to mix to a moist dough

Rub the lard into the flour and add the fruit. Mix in the honey and enough water to bind. Place this dough into a large cloth, such as muslin, and tie it tightly into a bag leaving a fold in the cloth so that the pudding can expand. Drop the cloth into a pot of boiling water and simmer for two or three hours until firm and cooked through. This should be a light pudding that has risen because of the wild yeast that is on the elderberries. Take out of the cloth, slice and serve with either butter or cream.

Oat and wheat nut dumplings

250g wholewheat flour
250g fine oatmeal
250g butter
125g chopped roasted hazelnuts
250g honey
1 pinch of salt
2 eggs
Milk to mix

Combine the flours and rub in the butter. Add the hazelnuts and stir in the honey and eggs. Add enough milk to make a soft dough. Put into a large muslin cloth as above and simmer in boiling water for three hours until cooked. Take out of the cloth, slice and spread with butter.

Seaweed pudding with elderflowers

$\frac{1}{2}$ cup of dried carragheen (*Gigartina mamillosa chondrus crispus*).
[This is a member of the dulse family and grows on the mid-shore rocks on the beaches around the British, French and Irish coasts. It can, however, be bought at most health food stores as 'Irish moss' or carragheen]
1 litre whole milk
1 sprig of elderflowers

Soak the dried seaweed in water for 10 minutes and drain. Add this to a pan of whole milk and add a sprig of elderflowers. Simmer for 30 minutes until the seaweed has dissolved, strain and pour into a bowl to set. Leave until it goes cold when it will have set like a jelly. Serve with a little honey if desired and some cream.

Seaweed pudding with blackberry juice

    1kg blackberries
    1 litre water
    ½ cup dried carragheen

Bring the blackberries and water to the boil in a pot and simmer for one hour. Strain and return fruit juice to the pot. Add the seaweed and simmer for another half hour until dissolved. Strain and pour into a bowl to set. When cold, this is a wonderful fruit jelly and can be served with cream. I am sure that in prehistoric times every possible use would have been made of this particular fruit. Its sweetness and flavour would have been eagerly awaited during the winter, spring and early summer months.

Fruit and cream

The simplest way to enjoy the wild fruit harvest is to just eat the fruit in a bowl and pour over some cream. The sweetness is provided by the fruit itself and just as relished today in our over-processed age as I am sure it was in the distant past.

Poppy seed and blackberry cake (53)

This is based on a continental recipe for poppy seed cake, using blackberries instead of candied peel.

    1½ cups poppy seeds
    6 eggs
    1 cup honey
    ½ cup of blackberries or any other fruit

Grind the poppy seeds between two stones or in a blender until you have flour. Beat the egg yolks until thick and, while beating, gradually add the honey. Stir in the blackberries and the ground poppy seeds. Beat the egg whites until stiff and fold into the mixture. Pour it into a lightly floured and greased dish and bake in a moderate oven for about 50 minutes. Allow the cake to cool in the dish, serve with fresh whipped cream.

Sweet bean cakes (colour plate 21)

>500g processed Celtic beans (see chapter 12 for processing recipe)
>500g wholewheat flour
>500g honey
>1 cup chopped hazelnuts
>250g butter

Rub the butter into the flour and add the beans. Stir in the honey and hazelnuts. Cook spoonfuls of the mixture on a hot griddle until light brown on both sides.

Glossary

Ard

The difference between a plough and an ard is that the plough has a mould board capable of turning over the earth. The ard, however, could only break up the soil. They were made of wood in various shapes but usually with stone ard points or stone shares which were attached to the tip of the beam to break up the earth.

Barrow

During the Bronze Age there was an increasing tendency towards single burials. Many of these tombs or graves were covered with a mound of earth known as a round barrow.

Beaker culture

These people are associated with the introduction of copper implements which are found in beaker burials. A typical feature of these burials is an inverted, bell-shaped beaker decorated with horizontal bands. These beakers are thought to have been made in order to trade some sort of alcoholic beverage.

Belgic Celts

Caesar reported the vast migrations of these people from mainland Europe to Britain in the first century BC. It is believed from the archaeological record that these people aggressively took the lands of south-eastern Britain as many hill forts were abandoned in southern Britain at this time. The Belgae adopted the Roman way of life more readily than the La Tène Celts in Britain. After the Roman invasion, they tended to live in or around Roman towns, making copies of Roman pottery and supplying the needs of the Romans for profit and favour.

Birch bark tar

The oldest finds revealing the use of wood tar in Europe were registered on a Middle Palaeolithic site in Germany. This was a period of the first tool-making and there was therefore a need for some sort of glue to haft axes and arrowheads onto wood. European Mesolithic sites reveal an abundance of artefacts which have remains of wood tar still on them, particularly on antler sickle hafts that had their flint inserts embedded in tar.

The production of birch bark tar involves the use of ceramics, as the bark has to be cooked in a sealed container in order to extract the tar. A wide pit is dug in the ground and a pot is placed in the centre. The pit has to be big enough for a fire to be lit which totally surrounds the central pot. On top of this lower pot, is placed another pot with holes in its base. It is into this pot that the peeled bark rolls are placed. A flat plate is put on top of the second pot and any cracks are sealed with fresh clay. A fire is slowly lit around the pot and gradually built up for a few hours when the tar from the bark in the top pot drips through the holes into the bottom pot. If there are any cracks in the seal, or if the fire is too hot, the tar vaporises and is lost. The mystery surrounding the production of birch bark tar is how did these people, before the Neolithic period and ceramic production, make this product without pots? At present, there is a great deal of research going on in Europe and America to find an answer to this question.

Bog body

A human corpse that has been preserved in waterlogged conditions so that the hair, skin, and sometimes the clothing, are preserved.

Bog butter

This is butter that has been stored in wooden containers in peat bogs to keep it fresh. The temperature of peat bogs remains cool in the summer so this feature was utilised by prehistoric societies to store their surplus butter until the winter.

Bronze Age

This period follows the Neolithic from 2,500-800 BC and sees the adoption of metalworking in northern Europe. The period began with copper-working, then developed into the manufacture of bronze alloy which is nine parts copper to tin.

Cairn

This is a mound of stones covering a burial or tomb.

Causeway camps

These sites date from around the early to late Neolithic period, approximately 4500-2500 BC. They are roughly circular areas, enclosed by between one to four concentric ditches with banks on their inner sides. These ditches were dug in irregular segments with 'causeways' of undisturbed earth between them. There seems to be little evidence for any fence or palisade on top of the inner bank. Apart from odd pits here and there and sporadically placed postholes, there seems to be no evidence for these camps having any permanent dwellings in them. They are built in a variety of situations — from the tops of hills to the bottoms of valleys and, in some cases, they are cut across the contours of a hill. However, there is quite a lot of debris in the ditches, such as animal bones, pottery and sometimes human bones.

There are many suggestions as to the possible use of these causeway camps: were they cattle compounds, centres for cult ceremonies, or places to meet and trade? I personally favour the latter. In the Neolithic period, communities would have been spread out in the countryside. A causeway camp could have been a meeting place at certain times of the year, either to trade or perhaps just meet up with the distant neighbours for a few days and share a meal or two. The animal bones in the ditches certainly indicate a large number of meals being eaten, particularly in southern Britain where lots of calf bones are found. Maybe in the springtime people gathered together to celebrate the end of winter and share their young calves in hearty feasts, then return home with their milk-laden cattle, refreshed until the next meeting, perhaps in the autumn. This could have been to perhaps swap rams or bulls and trade any produce they had made in the summer months. This is just my own theory but it seems as good an idea as any.

Chambered tombs

Chambered tombs consist of round, long, or other forms of barrows, which contain a burial chamber. A burial chamber strictly means the actual chamber in which the burials were deposited. Yet it is more generally used to describe the whole of the stone burial structure within a chambered tomb. The walls and passages of these tombs are made of either large stone slabs, or dry-stone walling. The inner roofs are made of layers of stone. These chambers were used for collective burials over a period of years during the Neolithic. When the last burial had taken place, the entrance was deliberately blocked and the whole tomb was covered with earth.

Cist

This is a small chamber made out of slabs of stone usually found under burial mounds.

Clome oven

This is a dome-shaped oven made of unfired clay and mud. It can have a hole at the top or not and is heated by a fierce fire of sticks within it for about an hour. This fire heats the thick walls of the oven so that when bread or meat are added and the openings are sealed, it cooks the contents. If there is a hole at the top of the oven, it makes it possible to cook some food in a pot on top while the main body of the oven is being heated for baking.

Corlea trackway

A great wooden trackway was uncovered at a bog in County Longford. This massive construction extended for 2 kilometres and was made of huge oak planks, 3.5-4m in length. These were laid down edge-to-edge on supporting pairs of longitudinal runners and made a broad, level wagon-way across the marshland. This trackway is dated to 148 BC and is one of the largest of its type in Europe.

Dugout canoe

A simple type of boat made from a single tree by burning and chopping out the centre.

Diodorus Siculus

This was a Roman historian from Sicily who wrote about many peoples in the classical world in AD 60. He wrote an account about the tin trade from Britain but mainly wrote about the Celtic peoples of Roman-occupied Europe.

Einkorn wheat

An early kind of wheat (*Triticum monococcum*) with one-grained spikelets, which was cultivated by the first farmers but is now only grown as animal fodder.

Emmer wheat

This is another ancient species of wheat grown in prehistoric times. However, it is thought to have been a hybrid between emmer and the hardy, wild goat-faced grass that produced the forerunner of bread wheats grown throughout the world today. This bread wheat was superior to emmer in several important ways, especially in that it did not have to be heated to enable the husks to be removed before grinding into flour. This new strain of wheat also had gluten which was lacking in the original strains. It was therefore possible to produce the light, yeasted breads we eat today.

Environmental archaeologist

These are specialists who study the environment at archaeological sites, mainly by identifying charred grains and by pollen analysis at various levels of an excavation. They also date wood finds by various methods, such as radio carbon dating and dendrochronology. The latter is a method of dating by counting tree rings; the process involves taking samples of different timbers of different ages and linking their growth patterns together with a series of a known date to provide an overall dating sequence.

Ertebolle culture

These settlements from Denmark are at the closing phase of the Mesolithic Stone Age. They are numerous and are known to occur in inshore waters as well as on the coastline. The characteristic features are the kitchen middens and transverse arrowheads — a new weapon at this time. The increasing importance of carpentry to these people promoted the development of larger shaped flint and greenstone axes. Fishing also seems to have grown increasingly important to these people as fish hooks and harpoon shapes are refined and fishing tackle is a common find at these sites.

Faience

A glazed, non-clay ceramic material widely used in Egypt for the production of jewellery. These beads, which are usually star-shaped or round, date to the earlier Bronze Age in Britain and are thought to have been manufactured in Britain.

Fogous and souterrains

Fogou is the name for an underground passage, lined and roofed in stone, which is usually attached to courtyard houses — a particular type of Iron Age settlement. Souterrain is the name for underground storage places in Scotland and Ireland. These stores are not always stone-lined but date from the same period.

Grauballe Man

This man, aged between 30 and 45, was discovered in 1952 in a peat-working in Denmark. He had died in the first century BC and had had his throat cut. He was so perfectly preserved by the peat that his red hair and the unshaved stubble on his face could still be seen. He was also thought to have been a man of high status, as his hands showed no sign of manual labour.

Hallstatt culture

The early Iron Age culture named after the burial ground at Hallstatt in upper Austria. They were primarily a salt mining people who dominated northern Europe from 800-400 BC.

Harpoon

A type of spear adapted for hunting fish which features barbs to prevent the point from being dislodged when the fish is pulled out of the water. They were typically made of antler horn or bone.

Hengistbury Head (Dorset)

This was a dominant port during the Iron Age, trading with Roman occupied Gaul. Here, metals from Wales, the Mendips and Cornwall could be stored prior to shipping to Amorica in France. It is possible that a substantial settlement surrounded this port to accommodate the traders, slaves and animals ready for export.

Herodotus

The Greek historian and author of nine books of histories, the main theme of which was the enmity and war between Persia and Greece. He lived in the fifth century BC.

Glossary

Hill fort

These were the fortified settlements found from the late Bronze Age to the Iron Age which were sometimes defended by multiple banks and ditches.

Ice Man

In 1991 a German couple, Erika and Helmut Simon, were enjoying a walking holiday in the Italian south Tyrol when they made an astounding discovery. They came across the body of a man which they thought was that of an unfortunate mountaineer. They had no idea that the body was of a Neolithic man 5300 years old. When this was discovered, a dispute broke out between the Austrians and the Italians to find which country he was in as he was almost exactly on the border. It was eventually confirmed that the body was 90m on the Italian side of a border which has shifted and changed constantly throughout the centuries. This was important to both Italy and Austria because of the effect such an important find could have on tourism. The Italians have since built a museum dedicated to the south Tyrol's archaeology and the Ice Man is the main exhibit — taking up the entire first floor of the museum. The body is kept in a specially made cold store, closed to the general public, which has a viewing window at the front. This is so that the public can see him while at the same time preserving the body in the right conditions. The wonderful part of this discovery is that he was a man caught out in the mountains, carrying normal day-to-day objects. When archaeologists find grave goods, it is hard to know if the items with a body are special or typical of everyday life; and goods found in middens are usually broken or useless.

His clothing is the most fascinating part of the find. He wore a long goatskin jacket made of alternate dark and light stripes of fur. His legs were covered with the sort of chaps that American Indians wear; they comprise two tubes for the legs with suspenders of strips of leather to hold them up. These were attached to a belt either side of a loincloth that looks just like the clothing of the Plains Indians in a Hollywood movie. On his feet, he wore shoes made of bearskin soles, red deerskin tops and the whole framework of the shoes were made from a net spun from the bark of the small-leafed lime tree. This net had grass stuffed inside instead of socks. Over his shoulders he wore a grass cloak made of wayside grasses held together with seven horizontal strips of lime bark string. He wore a bearskin hat and had a bow and quiver of arrows on his back. He carried a birch bark container in which it is believed from the evidence he kept the embers of a fire. He had a flint knife in a bark string scabbard on his belt.

Fascinating though this insight into his clothing was, nothing was quite so astounding as the copper axe he carried. This one find has pushed the age of metals in Europe back about 1000 years which is why the Ice Man is categorised as one of the greatest finds of the twentieth century. The museum also has a wonderful display of artefacts and reconstructions from the Stone Age, Bronze Age, Iron Age, the Roman period and the dark ages. So, if you happen to be in northern Italy or the Austrian Tyrol, it is well worth a visit.

Kimmeridge shale

Kimmeridge shale is a hard, black sedimentary rock upon which an industry was based in Dorset. Objects made from it were as varied as buttons, tabletops, plates, bracelets, spindle whorls and carvings. Many of these objects — particularly the bracelets — were made on a primitive lathe using flint-cutting tools.

La Tène culture

This Celtic culture appears in Europe around 400 BC and spreads from the Atlantic to the Black Sea. They are named after the site of a significant votive deposit on Lake Neuchatel in Switzerland. Lake dwellings such as the site at Glastonbury in Somerset are usually associated with these people. La Tène art is bold and abstract, with curvilinear designs and is the style we think of today as Celtic.

Lake villages

Settlements that were originally built at the edge of lakes or on islands as a defensive feature.

Lindow Man

In 1984 the well-preserved body of a man aged about 25 years was discovered in the peat of Lindow Moss in Cheshire. His body has been dated to the end of the Iron Age and he was the victim of murder, execution or sacrifice; he had been killed by blows to the head followed by garrotting.

Lunulae

From the beginning of the Bronze Age, these beaten gold collars are found in the shape of a crescent moon — hence the name. They were possibly symbols of status in a community as they are not found in graves, suggesting that they were passed on to the next generation after death. They are usually decorated with engraved geometric patterns.

Mesolithic

This period follows the Palaeolithic and the last Ice Age. These people subsisted through hunting, gathering and fishing and made distinctive harpoons and arrowheads from small flakes of flint called microliths.

Midden

Middens are rubbish-heaps mainly consisting of human food debris and other waste products. Some middens are made up entirely of shells, as every meal of shellfish generates large quantities of such waste. Bird, fish and domesticated stock bones are also common. Excavating these middens can tell the archaeologist not just what the people were eating, but also the size of the community and whether they lived on the site all year round or not.

Neolithic

The period of the first farmers, it follows the Mesolithic and sees the widespread adoption of permanent settlements and farming. This period also heralds the first manufacture of pottery and polished stone axes.

Nettle fibre

This is a fine, strong thread that is processed from our common stinging nettle. It is thought to have been the first thread to be spun and woven into cloth before linen and wool. There are finds of nettle fibre fishing net from the Neolithic levels of the lake villages of Switzerland. It is the bark of the stem that is used, being stripped off the main rib in late summer, boiled for hours in wood ash then rubbed with dry clay to remove the outer green filament.

[Upper] Palaeolithic

The beginning of this period 35,000 BC sees the first modern peoples appearing in Europe with advanced social structures and inventive tool manufacture. By 30,000 BC, the earliest cave art was painted in south-west France and northern Spain, and portable art objects were produced.

Pliny (AD 23-79)

Pliny the Elder, the Roman Historian who wrote the *Histories*, which are an account of all aspect of Roman life — from comments about the plundering of the planet's resources, to how to grow vegetables and medicinal remedies, to an account of the wild animals of Africa. If you get the chance, do read it as it is fascinating and very hard to put down. Pliny was on a ship in the bay of Naples when Vesuvius erupted. Due to his scientific curiosity, even though he was already safe, he re-landed on the shores of Herculaneum the next day and died from the volcanic gasses.

Pollen analysis

Grains of pollen often survive in certain conditions and can then be identified and counted under a microscope. From their types and relative abundance, a picture of the former vegetation in an area from which they came can be constructed.

Saddle quern

A saddle quern is the name for two stones that were used for grinding corn into flour in the Neolithic and Bronze Ages in Europe. The grain was placed on the lower large stone (the saddle stone) and a small top stone (the rider) is pushed to-and-fro on top of this. This quern was superseded in the Iron Age by the more efficient rotary quern, which consisted of a thick lower stone with a socket for a spindle on top, and a hemispherical upper stone with a socket for a handle. Grain was put in the top around the spindle. Using the handle on the top stone, a rotary action was used to grind the grain between the two stones and the flour came out of the sides of the convex base stone.

Spindle whorl

A small perforated disk of stone or ceramic which acts as a fly-wheel, maintaining momentum of the spindle for twisting fibres into thread.

Sprang

This is a textile technique that involves twisting strands of wool together, very much like the child's game of cats cradle. It is not weaving or knitting, as no extra threads are added during the process of making it. Sprang hairnets and bonnets have been found in several prehistoric graves in Denmark. The elastic quality of the sprang material makes it ideal for fashioning into bags or nets to contain moss for pillows, or straw for mattresses and is a much more economic use of spun thread than weaving. It is a technique that is still used by primitive cultures today.

Square-mouthed pot culture

An early Neolithic culture from northern Italy, thus named because of their pot-shaped and bowl-shaped vessels with a square, pinched mouth, yet with round bases.

Strabo (64 BC-AD 19)

The Greek historian and geographer native to Pontus in Asia Minor who wrote a geography of the Roman Empire.

Tacitus (AD 56-117)

The Roman historian, son-in-law of Agricola, and author of *Agricola*, which contains an account of Germania, histories and annals.

Tybrind Vig

This was a hunter-gatherer and fishing settlement off the coast of present-day Denmark. It was the first extensive underwater excavation in Denmark. Due to the favourable preservation conditions, cloth, string, rope and baskets from this period can be studied. Among the important finds was the Tybrind boat and decorated paddle which is dated to 4100 BC.

Tollund Man

Discovered in Denmark, this man had died in the second century BC by hanging and garrotting. He was found wearing a leather cap on his head, and his hands and nails indicated that he had not done any manual labour. Of all the bog bodies discovered in Europe that I have seen, he has the most peaceful look on his face — he looks just as if he is sleeping.

Warp-weighted loom

The typical type of loom used in prehistoric Europe is the warp-weighted loom. We know this because of the lines of weights excavated in dwellings and sometimes the remains of upright posts on either side of the weights are found. The process of weaving was very simple: the vertical warp threads were tied to stones or clay weights to keep them taught during the weaving process. These weights were supported by simple tree branches and, although it is easier to make small pieces of cloth by this technique, it is very simple and efficient.

Wattle and daub

This is the technique used to build the walls of many prehistoric dwellings. For example, when building a roundhouse, a circle of posts is first driven into the ground leaving a gap for the doorway. Thin hazel fronds or willow sticks are then woven between these posts to make a kind of continuous hurdle-like fence for the daub to adhere to. Daub is made by combining clay, earth and fibre with water. There are as many recipes for a good daub mix as there are roundhouse dwellings. My own mix for making daub is half river clay to soil, mixed with water and a few handfuls of straw to bind it all together. The clay must then be puddled. This process involves piling the above ingredients onto a flat area of ground and adding a few buckets of water; then comes the messy part. In order to make these ingredients into a sticky mass to apply to the walls it must be trodden (in much the same way as grape treading). It is best if two or three people link arms to stop from falling over and, with wellingtons or bare feet, proceed to stomp on the clay and soil pile. When well mixed, the daub then has to be thrown with some force into the ring of fencing, making up the outer walls of the dwelling. A final layer is then added and is smoothed over with the hands to make a wonderfully strong and insulated wall.

There are many who believe that cow manure must be added to make a good daub mixture because analysis has shown it to be the main ingredient in cob and daub walls. I believe that the cow manure could have been a by-product of the daub-making process and not necessarily an ingredient of the mix. If one is making a lot of daub to make a cob cottage, the simplest way to do this is make a small corral and add the clay and straw. Then put some cows in it for a few days and you will have perfectly mixed daub and, as a consequence of the cows' presence, a little cow manure to boot.

Another interesting result of making daub is the appearance of daubing pits. At archaeological sites where the walls of the houses are made of wattle and daub, there are often a number of pits next to each house. These pits have been called 'ritual pits' by archaeologists, as they appear to have no particular practical function. This is a prime example of experimental archaeology helping to solve these types of mysteries. When one makes daub on a flat area of ground next to the dwelling construction, each time the daub is removed to adhere to the walls, a little of the soil underneath is taken. After seven or eight mixes, a sort of accidental pit is formed. When the pit becomes too deep, it becomes difficult for the puddlers to get out, so a new flat area is selected to mix daub. Hence, there is a very practical reason for this row of ritual pits along settlement sites. As these pits are there after construction, they would maybe have been used for firing pots or cooking whole animals at a festival. If the daub mix were particularly clay-rich, the pit will fill with rainwater and form a pond. Many village ponds in cob built villages in the south of England were formed as a by-product of building the village itself.

Further reading

Andersen, S.H. (1985) 'Tybrind Vig: A Preliminary Report on a Submerged Ertebolle Settlement on the West Coast of Flyn'. *Journal of Danish Archaeology*, vol 4.
Audouze, F. & Buchsenschutz, O. (1991) *Towns, Villages and Countryside of Celtic Europe* (BCA, London).
Brzezinski, W. & Piotrowski, W. (1997) Proceedings of the First International Symposium on Wood Tar and Pitch (State Archaeological Museum, Warsaw).
Buckley, V. (1990) *Burnt Offerings: International Contributions to Burnt Mound Archaeology* (Wordwell Ltd.).
Coles, J.M. & Orme, B.J. (1982) *Prehistory of the Somerset Levels* (Stephen Austin & Sons Ltd.).
Dyer, J. (1990) *Ancient Britain* (Batsford).
Herodotus (Translation by Robin Waterfield 1998) *The Histories* (Oxford University Press).
Keating, G. (1908) *The History of Ireland*
Parker Pearson, M. (1996) *Bronze Age Britain* (English Heritage Publication).
Macready, S. & Thompson, F.H. (1984) *Cross-Channel Trade between Gaul and Britain in the Pre-Roman Iron Age* (Society of Antiquaries Publication).
Piggott, S. (1973) *Ancient Europe* (Edinburgh University Press).
Ross, A. (1970) *Everyday Life of the Pagan Celts* (Batsford).
Ryan, M. (ed.) (1991) *The Illustrated Archaeology of Ireland* (Country House Dublin).
Turner, R.C. & Scaife, R.G. (1995) *Bog Bodies* (British Museum Press).

Index

Index

Ash-cooked shellfish 124

Barley water 164
Bass stew with wild mushrooms 91
Bean and bacon stew 129
Beans and caraway 129
Beef and beer stew 91
Beer
    Meadowsweet ale 158
    Mild brown ale 157
    Nettle beer 159
    Spruce beer 158
    Strong ale 157
    Three flower beer 159
Beestings pudding 169
Birch sap wine 161
Bistort pudding 150
Blaand 165
Blackcurrant leaves 133
Black dumplings 170
Bog myrtle 137
Bread
    Autumn fruit bread 72
    Barley bread with beer 71
    Fresh fruit yeasted bread 72
    Malt bread (leavened) 69
    Malt bread (unleavened) 69
    Oat and barley bread 70
    Oatcakes 70
    Sweet bread 70
    Rich yeast spring bread 71
    Bread stones 97
Burdock 150
Butter making 81

Caraway 133
Celery, wild 148
Chervil 134
Chickweed 148
Chives 134

Dandelion and burdock 159

Elderflower champagne 161

Fat hen 146
Fish
    Bass stew with wild mushrooms 91
    Clay baked trout with ramsons 113
    Cod with mustard sauce 93
    Cod and oysters in beer 92
    Fish baked in clay 113
    King carp with wild plums 113
    Rollmops 92
    Smoked fish stew 92
    Soused fish in wine 92
Fruit and cream 172
Fruit dumplings 170

Hare stew 90
Hazelnut pancakes 170
Herb bennet 135
Horehound 135
Horseradish 135

Junket 169
Juniper 169

Lamb Stew 87
Lentils and fat hen or sea beet 131

Index

Lentil and mushroom soup 131
Linseed tea 164

Malt bread (leavened) 69
Malt bread (unleavened) 69
Malt (wheat) 69
Marsh thistle, braised 149
Meadowsweet ale 158
Meadowsweet 136
Mint 136
Mussels and bacon 124
Mussels in horseradish sauce 124
Mussel stew with dumplings 124
Mustard 136
Mutton stew 88
Mutton Stew with juniper berries 89
Myrtle pudding 108

Nettle beer 159
Nettle
    Creamed nettles 142
    Fried nettles 142
    Nettle oatcakes 142
    Nettle pudding no 1 107
    Nettle pudding no 2 108

Oat and barley bread 70
Oatcakes 70
Oat and myrtle cakes 137
Oat and wheat nut dumplings 171
Oyster and bacon kebabs 124

Pancakes 169
Parsley piert 138
Peas and apple 128
Peas (dried) with mint and cream 127
Pease pudding 128
Pigeon stew 89
Pignut 151
Poppy 138
Poppy seed and blackberry cake 172

Pork and beer stew 90
Pot boilers 96
Purple orchis 152

Ramsons 149
Rock samphire
    Beer and samphire pickle 144
    Fried rock samphire 144
    Samphire pickle 144
Rollmops 92

Salad vegetables
    Bedstraw 153
    Beech leaves 153
    Dandelion 153
    Flowers in salads 153
    Hawthorn leaves 153
    Jack-by-the-hedge 153
    Shepherd purse 153
    Sheeps sorrel 153
    Yarrow 153
Sandleek 138
Savoury bean fritters 130
Sea beet 145
Sea beet and cheese fritters 146
Sea beet greens 146
Sea kale 148
Seaweed pudding with elderflowers 171
Silverweed 151
Slackers 164
Sow thistle 144
Sow thistle greens 145
Spruce beer 158
Summer savoury 138
Sweet bean cakes 130
Sweet cicely 138
Sweet dumplings 170
Sweets and puddings
    Beestings pudding 169
    Black dumplings 170
    Fruit and cream 172

Fruit dumplings 170
Hazel nut pancakes 170
Junket 169
Oat and wheat nut dumplings 171
Pancakes 169
Poppy seed and blackberry cake 172
Seaweed pudding with blackberry juice 171
Seaweed pudding with elderflowers 171
Sweet bean cakes 173
Sweet dumplings 170

Tansy 139
Teas and soft drinks
    Blaand 165
    Barley water 164
    Linseed tea 164
    Slackers 164
Thyme 139

Vegetarian food
    Beans and caraway 129
    Breads 69-72
    Easter ledge or bistort puddings 150
    Dried peas with mint and cream
    Fried nettles 142
    Lentils and fat hen or sea beet 131
    Lentil and mushroom soup 131
    Myrtle pudding 108
    Nettle pudding no 1 107
    Nettle pudding no 2 108
    Nettle oatcakes 142
    Oat and myrtle cakes (using butter not lard) 137
    Peas and apple 128
    Pease pudding 128
    Sea beet and cheese fritters 146
    Sea beet and nut fritters 146
    Sea lettuce and curd cheese fritters 121
    Seaweed pudding 109

Savoury bean fritters 130
Soft cheeses 83-85
Sweet bean cakes 130
Vegetable stew 88

Wall pepper 139
Water lily 152
Water pit 102
Winkle butter 123
Wine
    Barley wine 163
    Birch sap wine 161
    Blackberry wine 162
    Elderflower champagne 161
    Elderberry wine 160
    English sack 160
    Metheglyn with caraway 162
    Rosehip wine 161

Yeast cycle 155